ELEMENTS

OF THE

CRITICAL PHILOSOPHY;

CONTAINING

A CONCISE ACCOUNT OF ITS ORIGIN AND TENDENCY;

A VIEW OF ALL THE WORKS PUBLISHED BY ITS FOUNDER,

PROFESSOR IMMANUEL KANT;

AND A GLOSSARY FOR THE EXPLANATION OF TERMS AND PHRASES.

TO WHICH ARE ADDED:

THREE PHILOLOGICAL ESSAYS;

Chiefly translated from the German of

JOHN CHRISTOPHER ADELUNG;

Aulic Counsellor and First Librarian to the Elector of Saxony.

BY

A. F. M. WILLICH, M. D.

LONDON:

PRINTED FOR T. N. LONGMAN,

No. 39. PATERNOSTER-ROW.

1798.

To

The REV. JAMES FINLAYSON, F. R. S. E.

Prof. of Logic and Metaphysics

in the University of Edinburgh;

And

The REV. JAMES MILNE,

Professor of Moral Philosophy

in the University of Glasgow:

These Elements

are

very respectfully inscribed

by

Their most obliged and humble Servant

The AUTHOR and TRANSLATOR.

To

The Right Honourable

SIR WILLIAM MILLER of GLENLEE, Bart.

One of the Senators of the

College of Justice

in Scotland:

PREFACE.

THE task of writing prefaces is none of the most grateful; especially when a variety of circumstances concur, to impose it as a duty upon one, who is in a manner, partly the author, and partly the translator of a new work, on a new subject.

It has now become the frequent practice of certain translators, to issue their mangled productions into the world as their own manufacture; though, upon comparison, they do not even deserve the character of being accurate translations from the German; a language, with which our modern translators, in general, are but very imperfectly acquainted.

To obviate a charge of this nature, and to acknowledge my obligations to those meritorious friends of literature in Germany, from whose labours I have derived very considerable assistance in the composition of this work, I must mention, in the first place, the REV. DR. STAEUDLIN, PROFESSOR OF DIVINITY AT GOETTINGEN. His classical performance, "*On the Spirit and History of Scepticism*, in two Volumes, octavo, 1794," has afforded me the materials of the 'HISTORICAL INTRODUCTION.'—In reliance upon a character of so much worth

PREFACE.

worth and eminence, as that of Dr. Staeudlin, I have not hesitated, pp. 23 and 24, to record, with due praise and respect, a work written by Mr. ADAM WEISHAUPT. Without entering upon an inquiry into Mr. Weishaupt's *moral* character I can safely aver, that his *literary* works have been received, upon the Continent, with almost universal approbation. In this assertion, I am supported by the Conductors of the first German Reviews in general, and particularly by the respectable evidence of Prof. Staeudlin himself, as well as by that of the celebrated PROF. EBERHARD of HALLE, both of whom have ranked Mr. Weishaupt's writings among the first philosophical compositions of Germany. And as he has lately published the third volume of his work " On Truth and Moral Perfection; Regensburg, 1796;" as likewise another work entitled, " On the secret Art of Governing; Frankfort on the Main, 1795;" I must leave Mr Weishaupt to defend his private character in Britain, as well as he has done it to the satisfaction of his learned friends in Germany.

For the conciseness of the ' SYNOPSIS,' which contains the statement and general solution of *Five connected Problems,* I need make no apology; as the terms occurring in this part of the ' ELEMENTS' are, I hope, sufficiently explained in the GLOSSARY. Without this expedient, I might have extended the Synopsis alone to a length, far exceeding the whole of the present work.

In the ' CHRONOLOGICAL ANALYSIS,' perhaps, I have been in some parts too prolix, while others might have

been

been enlarged upon with advantage. But it is not an easy matter to keep within proper bounds, in the discussion of abstract metaphysical subjects. Nor dare I flatter myself, that I am sufficiently acquainted with the idiom of the English language, to exhibit the most abstruse inquiries of the human mind, in a luminous point of view. In this respect, I can offer no better apology than that given by my great master, whose own words I have quoted in page 9. of the Introduction.—Although I had the good fortune to attend Prof. Kant's Lectures between the years 1778 and 1781, during my residence at the University of Koenigsberg; and again heard several of his Lectures in summer 1792, when I revisited my native country; yet I must confess, that my other professional labours have not permitted me to devote, to the study of the Critical System of Philosophy, that portion of time and close application, which, in more favourable circumstances, I should have been happy to bestow upon this important branch of human knowledge.

Relying, however, on the candour and impartiality of the learned in this country, I trust they will not decide upon a work of so comprehensive a nature as the present, from partial views; nor do I entertain the least apprehension, that they will be deterred from a *thorough* examination of it, by any *paradoxical* positions, or even *apparent* contradictions, that may occur in the *first* perusal.— A nation, which has produced a BACON, a NEWTON, a LOCKE, a HUME, and so many other *profound* inquirers, cannot be supposed to have a taste merely for the lighter,

(or

(or what are vulgarly called) *popular* pursuits of literature. Valuable and useful as these are to the community at large, no man of any penetration will deny, that metaphysical speculations, or inquiries into *first truths*, are equally beneficial and honourable; though they must ever remain the property of the few, whose genius leaves the beaten track, and searches for higher principles than such, as are barely deduced from the world of sense, or experience.

To those, therefore, who are both able and disposed to become acquainted with the spirit of the Critical System, I beg leave to address myself in the words of the worthy PROFESSOR WILL of ALTDORF, who gives his pupils the following excellent advice:

1. " Not to prejudge and decry the works of KANT, as being too subtle and abstruse, as being couched in unintelligible terms, as breathing innovation, and productive of confusion in philosophy:

2, " Not to complain of the want of that plainness, which is necessary to render a book palatable to *popular* readers; since difficulty of apprehension appears to be peculiar to the inquiries, that form the object of the ' CRITIQUE:'

3, " Not to appeal, according to the prevailing fashion of the age, to the decision of the multitude, whenever an abstract proposition occurs, which cannot, at first view, be clearly understood from the simple operations of *Common Sense;*' for Metaphysics do not acknowledge the *exclusive competency* of this tribunal:

PREFACE.

4, To abstract from all other Metaphysical Systems, in studying the Critical, i. e. not to make any other System the standard, by which the merits of the present are to be tried:

5, To study *first* the general aim of the work, by successively examining every solution, which the *Critique* of Kant affords in regard to the five principal problems (contained in the 'Synopsis'): and lastly,

6, As the inquiries forming the object of Kant's Critique are merely of a speculative nature, to proceed likewise in the prosecution of them merely upon speculative grounds, and to abstain carefully from all partial views of any interest whatever. For the result of sound speculation can never be prejudicial to the true interests of human nature."

With respect to the GLOSSARY, I must refer the reader to the few observations premised at the head of it: and if I have not succeeded in rendering the subject itself more intelligible, by the definitions given of those terms, in the use of which Kant differs from his cotemporaries, I can only plead the good intention, and the patient industry, with which I collected and arranged the materials.

The 'THREE PHILOLOGICAL ESSAYS' have been added to these 'ELEMENTS' by way of Appendix; in order to relieve the reader, in some degree, from the arduous task—and such it undoubtedly is—of reflecting upon so great a variety of abstract subjects. And as these Essays are, in a manner, unconnected with the Philosophy

of

of Kant, they have been at the same time separately printed, in a form somewhat different from the present; in order to accommodate those, who might wish to possess them as a distinct work.

Finally, the style and composition of this work, I am sensible, require more than common apology. Unfortunately, however, it is a matter of no small difficulty to make *good* apologies, especially in a foreign language. Whatever the execution may be, for the anxiety of my wishes I can confidently appeal to the testimony of those literary friends, who have occasionally lent me their aid in correcting the grammatical part of both the Elements and the Essays. They well know my eager and sincere desire of improvement in English composition; and if any material errors should occur in the course of such a diversity of subjects as the present, I beseech the judicious reader and the candid critic to consider, that I have ventured into a field of inquiry, of which but a small part has hitherto been explored.

The indulgence, which I claim, will not be withheld by those, who have tried their strength in translating from a foreign into their own language: and I apprehend still less severity from the few individuals, who have attempted to write, or to translate into, a foreign language, which they had an opportunity of acquiring, merely by reading and conversation.

NOVEMBER, 1797.

CONTENTS.

	PAGE
Historical Introduction, containing a succinct account of the origin and tendency of the Critical Philosophy,	1

ELEMENTARY VIEW OF THE PHILOSOPHY OF KANT:

Preparatory Remarks, — — — 34

I. SYNOPSIS.

   A. *Definition and Division of Philosophy,* — 38
   B. *Problems and Solutions:* Exordium, — 42
      Problem First, — — — 43
      Problem Second, — — — 44
      Problem Third, — — — 45
      Problem Fourth, — — — 49
      Problem Fifth, — — — 51

II. CHRONOLOGICAL ANALYSIS: Exordium, 53
   I. Reflections upon the true computation of living powers; 1746, — — — 55
   II.—XVI. A List of fifteen different works, which the author has published between the years 1755 and 1764, — — — 60
XVII. (1) *De Mundi sensibilis atque intelligibilis forma et principiis*; 1770, — — — 62
XVIII. (2) Critique of Pure Reason; 1781, — 64
  XIX. (3) Introductory observations with respect to every future System of Metaphysics &c. 1784, 80
   XX. (4) Reflections upon the foundation of the powers and methods &c. 1784, — 83
  XXI. (5) Fundamental Principles of the Metaphysics of Morals; 1785, — — *ibid.*
 XXII. (6) Metaphysical Principles of Natural Philosophy; 1786, — — — 93

XXIII.

CONTENTS.

		PAGE
XXIII. (7) Fundamental Principles of the Critique of Taste; 1787,		99
XXIV. (8) Critique of Practical Reason; 1788,		ibid.
XXV. (9) Critique of the Judging Faculty; 1790,		103
XXVI. On a certain discovery, &c. 1790,		113
XXVII. (10) Religion considered within the bounds of mere Reason; 1793,		114
XXVIII. Project for a Perpetual Peace; 1795,		121
XXIX. (11) Metaphysical Elements of Jurisprudence; 1797,		127
XXX. (12) Metaphysical Elements of Ethics; 1797,		134
A List of fourteen Essays, on various subjects, published by the author, between the years 1777 and 1794,		136
GLOSSARY:	from 139, to 183	

Corrigenda.

p. 16, l. 21 *for* directs, *read* deserts.

p. 19, l. 24, *for* Propedeutic, *read* Propædeutic.

p. 32, l. 23, *for* close, *read* those.

p. 83, l. 25, *for* inherent to, *read* inherent in.

Note: The terms *intuition* and *intuitive* have, by inadvertency, sometimes been used instead of the words, *cognition* and *cognitive*, particularly in No. XVIII. (2) of Kant's works, or between pp. 64. and 80.—The reader is therefore requested to attend to this circumstance, especially in places, where the promiscuous use of these terms might occasion some ambiguity.

ELEMENTS

OF THE

CRITICAL PHILOSOPHY, &c.

HISTORICAL INTRODUCTION.

IN Germany, two circumstances in particular have contributed to bring about a revolution in philosophy, and to diminish the estimation in which the *dogmatical system* of WOLF was formerly held: the study of the writings of the later English and French philosophers; and the appearance of a philosophic prince upon the throne of Prussia.

The former circumstance made the German philosophers acquainted with many objections that had been started against the dogmatical system of Metaphysics, gave rise to a turn for popularity in philosophical inquiries, and awakened a spirit of emulation among them. Selections were made from various systems; and the learned, now for the first time, began to convey information with elegance and taste. There arose a sort of *Eclecticism*, which discouraged party-spirit, and recommended philosophical discretion; but which was, at the same time, attended with some injurious effects; for incoherent systems were thus formed, inconsistent systems were mingled together, and philosophy became still more wavering and flimsy, and was still farther removed from the perfection of a science.

The history of philosophy was now investigated with greater attention, and more generally studied than it had formerly been:

been: With many, the study of philosophy was converted into that of its history;—a clear proof, how much the turn for dogmatism had declined, and how little hope was entertained of forming a system, at once stable and suited to the spirit of the age.

FREDERIC the Great collected a number of foreign philosophers round him, who, in a great measure, merely to pay adulation, and from selfish views, openly professed, like him, infidelity and scepticism. This circumstance, from the novelty of the thing, and from the admiration in which the character of Frederic was held, had an almost magical influence on all the opinions of the age. It would, however, be equal to ingratitude towards the manes of this surprising monarch, to omit mentioning in this place, that the system of his own practical philosophy has been held out, both by divines and laymen, as complete and downright Atheism; whereas it is now clear and uniformly admitted by sound and unprejudiced inquirers, that it amounted to nothing more than simple Deism.

Among the philosophers who surrounded Frederic, no one declared himself so expressly, and so openly, in favour of scepticism as d'ARGENS, the author of the "Philosophy of good "sense," which is written in a superficial manner, with a view of gaining popularity, but which is not even calculated for the Fair Sex and Gentlemen of fashion, for whose use it was originally designed; though it abounds in erudition and abstract speculation. D'Argens there endeavours to show the uncertainty of History, (and this is the best part of the work) of Logic, of Physics, of Metaphysics, and of Astronomy, without advancing, in opposition, any new, or genuine, philosophical principles. It does him, nevertheless, some honour that, with regard to the morality of life, he observes a respectful silence. His scepticism is directed more against the usual

pre-

pretenſions of the ſchools, and the learned in particular, than againſt human knowledge in general.

It is more remarkable, though leſs known, that, in the ſame country, a celebrated and profound Divine declared himſelf in favour of an almoſt unlimited *Pyrrhoniſm.*—M. de BEAUSOBRE, in his "Pyrrhoniſme raiſonable," called it rational, becauſe he allowed certain probabilities, both in kind and in degree, and maintained certain firſt principles, which did not admit of doubt. The work is written in a lively ſceptical humour, and affords pleaſure in the peruſal. It contains, indeed, many new and unexpected remarks; for it is an aſſault upon all ſyſtems, eſpecially upon that of Wolf. "ARISTOTLE," the author ſomewhere ſays, "had numerous followers for many centuries. The " time of his fall is now come; and DESCARTES has given him " the laſt blow. The fame of the French philoſopher was of " ſhorter duration, becauſe people now poſſeſſed more un-" derſtanding and leſs pedantry. LEIBNITZ came; Wolf " was his ſucceſſor: At preſent philoſophers are in a ſort of " anarchy; they wait for a man who is bold enough to build " upon the ruins of former Syſtems, new opinions, and conſe-" quently new errors." No where does Beauſobre attack religion and revelation, but rather reſpectfully affirms their certainty. The following paſſage is worthy of attention: "Al-" though it be difficult to prove the exiſtence of GOD by the " light of reaſon, yet even this light is ſufficient to convince " us, that the proof of the contrary is impoſſible. How can " we ſatisfactorily prove the oppoſite, if we have no clear idea " of the ſubject which we wiſh to call in queſtion? Although " I could bear in my mind no ſufficient proof of the exiſtence " of God, yet the advantage which attends the belief of this " truth, the impoſſibility of comprehending the nature of an " infinite Being, and the reflection that this truth is both the " moſt rational and uſeful of all others, would be ſufficient to

"induce any thinking person to give his assent, nay even to
"determine me."

But after this we are astonished to find him considering all morality as uncertain. His chief reason is, "that the good-
"ness of actions depends upon their consequences, which man
"cannot foresee, nor accurately ascertain." This argument, maturely considered, is obviously shallow, because it proceeds upon false ideas of morality: But the following objections are of greater importance: "That we are so little acquainted
"with the motives from which we act, and in general with
"our passions, that we know not how far our prejudices,
"and our weakness, can justify our actions; and that the in-
"terference and collisions of our different duties are inexpli-
"cable to most men, nay some of them inexplicable to all."
The remark at the end of this work is not less striking. "The
"uncertainty of our knowledge should not render us dissatis-
"fied; its advantage, or disadvantage, will not thereby be
"much affected. Certainty, with respect to us, is not even
"the most useful quality of our knowledge. The difficulty
"of acquiring accurate knowledge, is an admonition of nature,
"which reminds man of his weakness, and of the caution he
"ought to observe."

The inclination to Scepticism showed itself also in other parts of Germany, in different writings. It appeared mani-festly, for instance, in the "Physical Causes of Truth," by LOSSIUS, and in the first edition of PLATNER's "Philosophical
"Aphorisms." In the systems of Logic and elementary books also, much more regard was paid to it than formerly; in proof of which I shall only mention the excellent discussions in "LAMBERT's Organum," and in the elementary publications of FEDER.

But no author had, on the one hand, paid more attention to the objections of the Sceptics, and the distinguishing character-
istic

HISTORICAL INTRODUCTION.

istic of the possible systems; and on the other, investigated more profoundly the faculties of the Human Understanding, and, indeed, of the whole Human Constitution, than TETENS, in his "Philosophical Inquiries concerning Human Nature, and the "developement of it," which were published in two volumes, in the year 1777. It is not our business here to mark minutely the excellencies or defects of this work; we take notice of it on this account chiefly, because that profound philosopher was the first among the Germans, who examined some of the ideas of HUME, with an acuteness worthy of such an opponent; and he has investigated the doctrines of *objective* truth, and of the objective existence of things, more deeply and more precisely than had been done before. Against the explanation given by Hume, of the idea of Causation, he objected with justice, that it did not exhaust the subject; for we understand by it not merely a connection, but also a dependence of one thing upon another. He remarked that we perceive in ourselves ideas in a necessary succession, and that this is properly our notion of a cause, or connection: he pointed out instances, in which the subjective connection of ideas arises from a necessary operation of the understanding, and, actually, has another foundation than the association of ideas formed by experience;—cases where we explain a compound effect from compound causes; and where the idea of the complex effect has never been before associated with that of the complex cause, but where the connection is the work of reflection: in fine, he has pointed out the operations of the mind, by which we deduce one truth from another. He maintained, therefore, that the idea of Causation is abstracted from certain associations of ideas, in which we remark something more than mere succession and combination.

Although this explanation is not altogether satisfactory, yet it, in a great measure, holds good against Hume's idea. Tetens
admits

admits that sensations afford the materials for all ideas; but he contends that *their* form depends upon the mind, or the power of thinking. After having, in a very profound manner, illustrated the origin of our knowledge, from the objective existence of things, he next examines the truth of objective knowledge. According to his acceptation of the terms, our knowledge is called objectively true, in so far as objects must be perceived by every other being, in the same manner in which we represent them to ourselves;—a being who has such a mind as we have: and in so far as the relations, which we remark in our external perceptions, correspond with those of every other being, whose understanding is so constituted, that it thinks of the objects in question, as we do. The necessary rules of thought, according to which the mind proceeds, are, with him, not only *subjective* rules of our thinking faculty, but of every reflecting principle; and the general truths of reason are not only truths with respect to us, but to every reasoning being. We cannot conceive an understanding which is capable of thinking against the principle of contradiction, or in other words, of disputing the admissibility of that principle: hence this is justly considered as an objective principle.

Tetens here contradicts what Lossius had laid down; and what Descartes had indeed, pretty distinctly before explained: That truth is only a relation with respect to the being who thinks of it, and that the contradiction is incapable of being an object of thought, only with respect to our understanding. Thus Tetens, with many others, proceeded in reasoning upon subjective necessary principles. He appealed to the fact, that when we apply theories to real objects, we always suppose that the reality is so constituted, as the general ideas represent it. But here, argues he, the mind proceeds according to laws which we must consider as the laws of every reasoning being;

being;—consequently the truths which are here admitted, or supposed, are objective truths.

With respect to the objects of sense, the knowledge of them, indeed, is often only an objective appearance; but the necessary laws of thought lead to this conclusion, that other thinking beings, in similar circumstances, represent these objects to themselves in a similar manner; that these objects, with certain conformations, exist without us, and that certain properties of the impressions which we experience, are also the properties of the objects themselves.—A Sceptic, however, without going out of his way in quest of far-fetched arguments, might easily find a good deal to object against this deduction.

The work of Tetens had not the effect of promoting a solid philosophic spirit, and of bringing about a salutary revolution in the study of philosophy, which might otherwise have been expected. But this was not merely the consequence of the circumstances of the times;—but also of a stile, not so much obscure, as languid, prolix and affected; as well as of a slavish dependence upon the Empiricism of Locke, which is insufficient for the explanation of the most important problems.

What this work did not accomplish, another did.—KANT, who by various compositions upon philosophical subjects, had long ago announced himself as an original genius, and an excellent philosopher, published in the year 1781, the "Critique of Pure Reason," which promised a total and beneficial reform in every philosophical department. For a long time, however, after its publication, it had been unaccountably neglected, or, at least, misunderstood. This was surely not in consequence of the difficulties, with which the study of it, as well as of every metaphysical subject, is necessarily attended; but of a certain indifference to philosophy, and of a rooted taste for shallow and popular discussions, which Kant directly opposed. But as soon as the work was more studied and investigated

gated, and had found several successful Commentators, at once a revolution in philosophy commenced. It soon met with numerous admirers and friends, and even its opponents could not with-hold their admiration from this masterly production. They saw themselves, every where, driven from their strong holds, and obliged to erect new fortifications for the defence of those philosophical tenets which they wished to maintain. Nay, many of the enemies of this system became its friends; and the invaluable part of it, which treats of morals, met with an almost universal approbation. All the different branches of Philosophy were examined with greater ardour, and new sources of knowledge, which formerly had scarcely been conceived, were now exposed to view. The limits of the science were more accurately defined, and the laudable researches after stable and simple principles, and after a rigid method, gave to philosophical inquiries a certainty, and an interest, which for a long time they had not possessed. Long before this period doubts had arisen, in reflecting minds, concerning the systems of Leibnitz, Wolf and Locke; but these had never been unfolded with sufficient clearness, nor a better system substituted in the place of that which was to be relinquished. Here all systems were examined with critical acumen, and a solid foundation was laid for a new one. This New Philosophy, in a short time, was attended with an almost magical influence upon all the Sciences. It found friends and adherents, even among ranks of people who had not devoted themselves to Science, or least of all, to Metaphysics. It excited in Germany, a sound, philosophic spirit of inquiry, of which the present age was scarcely deemed capable. It contains such an immense store of new ideas and views that, hitherto, only a small part of these materials can be considered as digested, and even, in a distant age, new branches of knowledge may shoot forth from it.

The

The work itself is arranged with a systematic spirit, and written with a noble philosophic impartiality. The style is somewhat obscure *, the construction and arrangement of the periods, in many places, ungraceful, heavy, and over-loaded; but a reader who has a tolerable understanding, and an interest for truth, is sufficiently recompensed by the originality of thought, and by the new and striking images in which it abounds. The celebrated author discovers all the talents requisite to a reformer of philosophy, especially in our age:—not merely an admirable acuteness, and a rare talent of making *himself* the object of *his* reflection, but also a knowledge in Mathematics and Natural Philosophy, of which he had formerly given proofs: a nice sensibility of the Beautiful and Sublime; and in general, a cultivated manly taste, a thorough acquaintance with the different Systems of philosophy that prevailed before his time; and a refinement of feeling, which is truly honourable.

It is not my design *here*, to describe minutely the system of this philosopher, which, besides the work already mentioned, is explained in the " Prolegomena to every future System of Metaphysics," published in 1783; in the " Fundamental Principles of the Metaphysics (Theory) of Morals," in 1785; in the " Metaphysical Principles of Natural Philosophy," in 1786; in the " Critique on Practical Reason," in 1788; in the " Critique on Judgment," in 1790; and in the " Religion within the limits of Pure Reason," in 1793: And which System has found in REINHOLD, SCHULZ, SCHMID, and others, friends and commentators,—men who themselves were qualified

B

fied

* " I am not very conscious," says KANT, in his preface to the 2d edition of the *Critique of Pure Reason*, p. 43. " that I possess the talent of exhibiting an abstract philosophical subject in a luminous point of view: I trust that the occasional defect of style will be further supplied by the writings of those deserving characters who, together with a solid judgment, are in the possession of that talent. For, this being the case, there is no *danger* of being refuted, but rather of being *misunderstood*.

fied to advance science. The following abstract will be sufficient for our present purpose.

Kant begins with doubting, whether Metaphysics, in general, be capable of being studied as a science. He remarked that, hitherto, this branch of knowledge could not lay claim to the appellation of a science; although it was older than all the others, and besides, by the interest it excited, always obtruded itself upon our attention. Two circumstances led him to discoveries, which were to bring about a revolution in Metaphysics, and secure to them the rank of a science;—the observation, by what means Mathematics and Natural Philosophy had become sciences; and Hume's inquiries concerning the idea of causation. We begin with the latter, and shall make Kant himself give the account of it.

" Since the Essays of Locke and Leibnitz, or rather since
" the origin of Metaphysics, as far as their history extends, no
" circumstance has occurred, which might have been more
" decisive of the fate of this science, than the attack which
" David Hume made upon it. He brought, indeed, no light
" into this department of knowledge, but he struck a spark
" which, if it had fallen among combustible materials, and had
" been carefully fanned, might have been easily kindled in-
" to a blaze. Hume proceeded upon a single but important
" idea in Metaphysics, the connection of cause and effect, and
" the concomitant notions of power and action: he challenged
" *reason* to answer him, what title she had to imagine, that any
" thing may be so constituted as that, if it be given, something
" else is also thereby inferred: for the idea of cause denotes
" this. He proved beyond contradiction, that it is impossible for
" reason to think of such a connection *a priori*, and out of
" its own ideas; for it contains necessity; but it is not pos-
" sible to perceive how, because something is, something else
" must

"must also necessarily be; nor how the idea of such con-
"nection can be introduced a priori."

"Hence he concluded, that reason entirely deceives herself
"with this idea, and that she erroneously considers it as her own
"child, when it is only the spurious offspring of imagination,
"which imagination, impregnated by experience, has brought
"certain ideas under the law of association, and substituted a
"subjective necessity, thence arising, that is habit, for an ob-
"jective one derived from perception. Hence, again, he con-
"cluded that reason had no title to think of such connections,
"even in a general manner; because then all her general ideas
"would be merely fictions, and all her pretended notions,
"stamped a priori, would be nothing else than counterfeited
"ordinary lessons of experience: which is just saying, there is
"no science of Metaphysics at all, and there can be none."

"However hasty and unwarrantable Hume's conclusion
"might appear, yet it was founded upon investigation, and this
"investigation well deserved, that some of the philosophers of
"his time should have united to solve more happily, if pos-
"sible, the problem in the sense in which he delivered it: a
"complete reform of the science might have resulted from
"this solution. But it appears to have been the unavoidable
"destiny of Metaphysics, that *he* should not be understood by
"his cotemporaries. For it is a mortifying reflection, that *his*
"opponents, REID, BEATTIE, OSWALD, and lastly PRIESTLEY
"himself, totally misunderstood the *tendency* of his problem.
"Always admitting as granted, what he never had called in
"question, they so misunderstood his aim at improvement, that
"every thing remained in the same state, as if nothing had been
"done.—The question was not, whether the idea of cause be in
"itself proper, and indispensible to the illustration of all natural
"knowledge; for this Hume had never doubted; but whe-
"ther this idea is an object of thought through reasoning a
priori;

" priori; and whether, in this manner, it possess internal evi-
" dence, independently of all experience; consequently, whe-
" ther it be of such extensive utility, as is not limited to objects
" of sense alone.—It was upon this point Hume expected an
" explanation.

" The opponents of this celebrated man, in order satisfac-
" torily to solve *his* problem, would have been under the ne-
" cessity of penetrating more profoundly into the abstract na-
" ture of reason, in so far as it is employed in *pure* thought;
" an inquiry to which *they* were little, if at all, disposed.—
" Hence they contrived a more convenient method of display-
" ing their malignity, without subjecting themselves to the
" trouble of making further researches; namely, the appeal
" to the *common sense of mankind*.—It is indeed a great gift of
" Heaven, to possess a plain and unbiassed understanding;—
" but we must manifest it, and establish ourselves in this pos-
" session, by facts, by reflection, and by reason, by what we
" do and say; not by appealing to it as an oracle, when we
" can produce no rational arguments to justify the claim.—
" When observation and science are put to the last shift, then,
" and not sooner, is it time to appeal to common sense.—
" This is one of the subtle contrivances of modern times, by
" which the shallow prattler assumes a right, boldly to chal-
" lenge a man of profound erudition, and frequently main-
" tains the contest. As long, however, as there is any room
" left for discovery, we shall do well to beware of having re-
" course to this last expedient. And, in truth, this appeal is
" nothing else than a submission to the judgment of the mul-
" titude, a reference at which the Philosopher blushes, but in
" which the silly witling triumphs and exults.—I should
" think, too, Hume might have laid claim to a sound un-
" derstanding, as well as Beattie; and besides, to what the
" latter certainly did not possess, to a critical acquaintance with
" that

" that species of reasoning, which keeps common sense within
" due bounds, and prevents it from losing itself in speculat-
" tions; or what is more to the present purpose, which hin-
" ders it from deciding upon any subject, because it knows not
" how to justify its mode of proceeding upon its own prin-
" ciples; a restraint, without which an understanding will
" not long remain sound.—The chissel and the mallet may do
" well enough for shaping a piece of timber, but the ra-
" dius-needle, a nicer instrument, must be employed for en-
" graving.—In the same manner, a sound and plain under-
" standing, as well as a speculative one, are each of use in
" their turn; the former, when we are conversant about
" judgments that are immediately applicable to experience;
" the latter, when we are about forming general judgments
" from mere abstract ideas, as in Metaphysics, where the un-
" derstanding, termed sound or plain, but often erroneously so
" denominated, cannot afford any assistance.

" I freely own, the suggestions of David Hume were, what
" first, many years ago, roused me from my dogmatical slum-
" ber, and gave to my inquiries quite a different direction in
" the field of speculative Philosophy.—I was far from be-
" ing carried away by his conclusions, the fallacy of which
" chiefly arose from his not forming to himself an idea of the
" *whole of his problem*; but merely investigating a part of it,
" the solution of which was impossible, without a comprehen-
" sive view of the whole.—When we proceed upon a well
" founded, though not thoroughly digested thought, we may
" expect, by patient and continued reflection, to prosecute it
" farther, than the acute genius had done, to whom we are in-
" debted for the first spark of this light.—I first enquired,
" therefore, whether Hume's objection might not be a general
" one, and soon found, that the idea of cause and effect is far
" from being the only one, by which the understanding a
priori

"priori thinks of the connection of things; but rather, that
"the science of Metaphysics is altogether founded upon these
"connections.—I endeavoured to ascertain *their* number, and
"as I succeeded in this attempt, upon a *single principle*, I pro-
"ceeded to the deduction of those general ideas which, I was
"now convinced, are not, as Hume apprehended, derived
"from experience, but arise out of the pure understanding.
"This deduction, which seemed impossible to my acute pre-
"decessor, and which nobody besides him had ever conceived,
"although every one makes use of these ideas, without asking
"himself, upon what their objective validity is founded; this
"deduction was, I say, the most difficult which could have been
"undertaken for the behoof of Metaphysics. And what was
"still more embarrassing, Metaphysics could not here offer me
"the smallest assistance, because that deduction ought first to
"establish the possibility of a system of Metaphysics. As I
"had now succeeded in the explanation of Hume's problem,
"not merely in a particular instance, but with a view of the
"whole power of pure reason, I could advance with sure,
"though tedious steps, to determine completely, and upon
"general principles, the compass of pure reason, both what
"is the sphere of its exertion, and what are its limits: which
"was all that was required for erecting a system of Meta-
"physics upon a proper and solid foundation."

Kant remarked, that Mathematics and Natural Philosophy had properly become sciences by the discovery, that reason a priori attributed certain principles to objects; and he inquired, whether we could not also succeed better in Metaphysics by taking it for granted, that objects must be accommodated to the constitution of our mind, than by the common supposition, that all our knowledge must be regulated according to external objects. The following are the elements of his "Critique of pure reason,"—the first of Kant's systematical works,

works, and the most remarkable for profound reasoning, and the striking illustrations, with which it throughout abounds:

"We are in possession of certain notions a priori, which are absolutely independent of all experience, although the objects of experience correspond with them; and which are distinguished by necessity and strict universality. To these are opposed empirical notions, or such as are only possible a posteriori, that is, through experience. Besides these, we have certain notions, with which no objects of experience ever correspond, which rise above the world of sense, and which we consider as the most sublime, such as *God, Liberty, Immortality.*—There are *analytical* and *synthetical* judgments a priori; the former are merely illustrative, and depend upon the principle of contradiction; the latter are *amplificatory*, i. e. they enlarge our knowledge, and are established upon another (assertory) principle. The last are peculiar to the science of Metaphysics; although it also contains analytical judgments. Besides, there are contained in all theoretical sciences of reasoning, purely synthetical judgments a priori as principles, namely, such as amplify, or enlarge our knowledge of objects, without immediate perception.—Mathematical judgments are altogether synthetical. The Mathematician may by his position always give something material, or empirical; but there is always supposed in it a pure perception a priori, a form of the sensitive faculty, viz. *Space* and *Time*. This form first renders every actual appearance of objects possible. Thus pure Mathematics are possible, and can be reduced to a scientific form—Natural Philosophy also contains synthetical judgments a priori, as its principles.—By the sensitive faculty we are able to form perceptions: by the understanding we form general ideas. By the sensitive faculty we experience impressions, and objects are given to us: by the

"the understanding we bring representations of these objects
"before us; we think of them. Perceptions and general
"ideas are the elements of all our knowledge. Without the
"sensitive faculty, no object could be given (proposed to)
"us: without the understanding, none could be thought of
"by us. These two powers are really distinct from one ano-
"ther; but neither of the two, without the other, can pro-
"duce a *notion*, (*Erkenntniss*). In order to obtain a distinct
"notion of any one thing, we must present to our general ideas,
"objects in perception, and reduce our perceptions to, or con-
"nect them with, these general ideas.—As the sensitive fa-
"culty has its determined forms; so has our understanding,
"likewise, forms a priori. These may be properly termed
"*Categories*; they are pure ideas of the understanding, which
"relate, a priori, to the objects of perception in general. The
"objects of experience, therefore, are in no other way pos-
"sible; they can in no other way be thought of by us;
"and their multiplied diversity can only be reduced to
"*one* act of judgment, or to one act of consciousness, by
"means of these Categories of sense. Hence, the Catego-
"ries have objective reality.—— They are either **Catego-**
"ries of 1. *Quantity*; as unity, number, totality: or 2. of
"*Quality*; as reality, negation, limitation: or 3. of *Rela-*
"*tion*, as substance and accident, cause and effect; or the re-
"ciprocal operation between agent and sufferer: or 4. of
"*Modality*; as possibility and impossibility, existence and
"non existence, necessity and contingency.—The judgment is
"the capacity of applying the general ideas of the under-
"standing to the information of experience. *) The objects of
"experience are regulated according to these ideas; not, vice
"versa

---

* Hence we observe in those who are deprived of, or deficient in, this important faculty, that they are unable to determine between good and bad, between danger and safety, and so forth.

" verfa, our ideas according to the objects. We can attain no
" knowledge of an object, as a thing in itfelf, but only fo far
" as it is an object of our fenfitive perception, or a phenome-
" non; though we muft be capable of conceiving objects as
" fubftances, and likewife of admitting their reality; becaufe
" our *internal* experience, the confcioufnefs of our own ex-
" iftence, is only poffible on the fuppofition of *external* expe-
" rience, or by the perception of other things without us.
" As foon as we pretend to confider the objects of fenfe, as
" things in themfelves, reafon falls into a contradiction with
" itfelf, into oppofite principles which it cannot unravel; fo
" that as much can be faid for one pofition, as for its oppofite.
" Our knowledge, then, is wholly confined to the objects of
" experience, without which the pure abftract ideas of the
" underftanding are of no value, and confequently they are
" no longer of ufe, when we abandon the regions of the *fenfi-*
" *ble* world. Liberty, God, and Immortality are ideas which
" are exalted above all fenfitive faculties; they are not ob-
" jects of fenfitive knowledge, nor of objective certainty, but
" of *neceffary* thought and belief. *Speculative* reafon, when it
" confiders any thing, as to what it *is in itfelf*, directs us here,
" or leads us into conjecture and contradiction; but *practical*
" reafon, when it confiders that which *fhall be*, by clear ex-
" preffions announces to us truths, than which nothing can
" be more important. It declares us, as moral beings, to be
" free agents, who are not fubjected to the mechanifm of na-
" ture: it holds out to us an *ideal*, moral perfection, which
" we *ought* to attain, but which we *can* attain only by an
" endlefs progreffion, and therefore enjoins us to cherifh a be-
" lief in immortality. By the idea of a moft perfect ftate, it
" fatisfies that inftinctive defire of happinefs, which is a con-
" ftituent part of our fenfitive nature; and while it holds out
" to us the idea of a moft *perfect harmony*, in which happinefs

" and virtue must one day be united; it teaches us to believe
" in the existence of that Being, who alone can establish this
" harmony."

This imperfect account will, at least, serve the purpose of shewing, how this system, on the one hand, sets limits to the *Scepticism* of Hume; while it refutes and overturns *Materialism, Fatalism, Atheism*, as well as *Fanaticism* and *Infidelity*.—Kant does not attack the dogmatical process of reason employed in pure (abstract) notions, but rather enjoins so far a more strict dogmatism than formerly prevailed, while he raises Metaphysics to the rank and solidity of a science: he combats that arrogant dogmatism, which sets out with its *hypothetical* notions, without previous enquiries, whether, and how far reason is intitled, by its peculiar judging powers, either to admit, or to reject, these notions. " This critical work of mine," he says, " is not written with a view of encouraging prat-
" tling shallowness, under the arrogant name of popularity,
" nor for the purpose of supporting scepticism which, as well
" as the former, is rather an excrescence, than an ornament of
" the sciences. The *Critique* is the previous preparation for
" the advancement of a well-founded system of Metaphysics,
" as a science which, necessarily dogmatical, and in the strict-
" est sense systematic, must be formed according to scientific
" rules, not merely adapted to the vulgar."—Upon Scepticism, its value, its limits, its relation to the Critical Philosophy, Kant, in another part of his inquiry, has made excellent remarks.—JACOB, another German Philosopher, has since, in a more direct and comprehensive manner than Kant himself, employed the Critical Philosophy for the confutation of Scepticism in general, and that of Hume in particular.

Not long after Kant's Critique, there appeared a work, by an ingenious and liberal author, " upon the doctrine of Spinoza, in Letters to Moses Mendelssohn, 1785, which accidentally, in many instances, confirmed the doctrines of the Critique. The author defined *belief* to be immediate certainty, which required no support by arguments, superseded all proofs, as it rested upon a revelation, and contained the elements of human knowledge; he maintained, that reason only leads to doubts and errors in the most important objects of thought, that Spinozism is still the most coherent system of reasoning, but it establishes downright atheism; and that in general, according to the expression of PASCHAL, "*Reason exposes the Dogmatist to shame, and nature itself refutes the Sceptic.*"—As little however, as his doctrines of belief agree with the principles of Kant, so much were his opinions, of Scepticism and Spinozism, a strong corroboration of Kant's assertions; that *speculative* reason teaches us *nothing*, with demonstrative certainty, upon the existence of God, and the objects beyond the world of sense. —Soon after this, in 1787, the worthy son of a truly philosophical father, Joh. Albr. Heinr. REIMARUS of Hamburgh, published a work " upon the foundation of human knowledge, and natural religion," in which he examines the different doctrines of Jacob and Kant, and which here deserves honourable mention, as it contains many valuable hints, together with happy illustrations of interesting, though abstruse, subjects. In the mean time Kant's system, or rather his elementary *Propedeutic* for a system, acquired still greater reputation, and gained every where friends notwithstanding several accidents of so serious a nature, as to threaten its subversion. The system of Locke, that of Leibnitz, a species of Eclecticism, and finally the Philosophy of Common Sense, were alternately opposed to it. Some imagined they saw in it a concealed infidelity; others an over-credulous religious and moral *Mysticism*; a third party maintained, that it led to Scepticism; and a fourth, that it contained nothing new. All these obstacles could not retard the rapid progress it was daily making, almost without exception, in the Protestant Universities of Germany: in many of the Catholic Schools, too, it obtained decisive victories over the systems of Aristotle and Descartes.

But however much, from conviction, enlightened minds were inclined to befriend this philosophy, yet with a moderate acquaintance with the history of Ethics, it was easy to foresee, that even Kant's System, notwithstanding all the evidence and strength of its principles, could scarcely withstand the furious attacks of Pyrrhonism, or rather the pyrrhonic art, by which, without discrimination, every thing is called in question; Mathematics and Natural Philosophy itself not excepted. Without doubt, many of the opponents of the New Philosophy, long ago remarked this; but they hesitated to make the pyrrhonic experiment with Kantianism; because every other possible system, that could be substituted in the room of the Critical, might in like manner be rendered wavering and uncertain; and because such a pyrrhonism, in general, either leads to no end at all, or it is attended with consequences detrimental to morality and happiness.—Further, this attack would only have served to place the strength of the system attacked, in a more striking point of view.—But a more moderate scepticism might have been easily and advantageously employed against certain principles of the Critical Philosophy, if its opponents had been aware of denying, or calling in question, some facts of consciousness, to which Kant necessarily appeals. It was not, therefore, a matter of surprise that, after repeated attacks in our times, this species of scepticism also should be employed against the Critical Philosophy.

The author of " Aenesidemus," or, on the foundation of the " Elements of Philosophy, published by Prof. Reinhold, in " Jena; together with a defence of Scepticism, against the " pretensions of the Critical Philosophers, 1792," has endeavoured to prove, that the sceptical doctrines of Hume are

not

not in the least confuted by the Critique of Pure Reason. The work, here mentioned, is written with uncommon perspicuity, acuteness, and respect towards the Father of the Critical Philosophy. The anonymous author directs his objections against the chief pillars of Kant's System, the derivation of necessary synthetical judgments from the mind, and the reference of these to the perception of *empirical* objects. He allows, that there are necessary synthetical judgments in human knowledge, that they form an indispensible part in it, and that the necessity which takes place in the connection of the predicate with the subject, in these judgments, can be derived neither from pre-existence, from frequent repetition, nor from the conformity of a certain number of facts. But he maintains, that, in the " Critique of Pure Reason," the mind is held out as the real ground of these necessary judgments, that from our being able to think only of the power of representation (or conception) as the foundation of necessary synthetical judgments, a conclusion is drawn, that the mind *must actually be* the foundation of these. Now, argues he, what Hume called in question, is here plainly taken for granted; namely, 1st, that for every thing we perceive, there is objectively pre-existing a real ground, and a really distinct cause of it, so that the position of the sufficient ground, in general, depends not only upon the representations and their subjective association, but also upon *things in themselves*, and their objective connection: 2dly, that we are intitled, from the constitution of a something in our conception, to form conjectures respecting the constitution of that something without us.—Kant, continues this Sceptic, has not proved, that our mind alone can be the ground of synthetical judgments; for the consciousness of necessity, which accompanies these judgments, is not an infallible criterion of their origin a priori, and from the mind.—That we *cannot* now think of, or explain something otherwise but in a certain manner;

hen; this circumstance by no means proves, that we *could not* have thought of it in any other way. Another origin of these judgments is conceivable, than from the mind; namely, from the operation of real objects, and their various modes of affecting us. It might, therefore, be eafily conceived, that reprefentations and general ideas, which exift in us a priori, are ftill in another way referable to real objects, than merely by the circumftance, that they exhibit to us the conditions and forms of the objects. Thefe reprefentations and ideas a priori, might alfo relate to the objective conftitution of things without us, by means of a pre-eftablifhed harmony between thefe, and the operations of our underftanding; and agreeably to this harmony, fomething might be reprefented to the mind by means of perceptions and general ideas a priori, which fhould not only have objective validity in our underftanding, but alfo correfpond with the conftitutions of things in themfelves, and be the means of reprefenting them.—The Critical Philofophy, he adds, proves the origin of neceffary fynthetical judgments from the mind, by making fuch ufe of the principle of caufation, as is contrary to its own principles in the application of the Categories; whether we underftand by mind a *Noumenon*, a thing in itfelf, or a tranfcendental idea.—To thefe doubts, feveral of which were formerly propofed by FLATT and BRASTBERGER, the friends of the Critical Philofophy have already anfwered. Whether the fcepticifm of this author agrees with that of Hume, whether it does not contain in feme refpects more, in others lefs than the laft, I fhall not venture to determine.

PLATTNER, that excellent *Anthropologift*, who, in a rare inftance, to a profound knowledge of medicine, joins extenfive erudition in philofophy, and peculiar penetration, and who deferves to be ranked among the firft philofophers of Germany, has employed rational fcepticifm againft the Kantian Syftem,

in

in an elementary treatise, designed chiefly for academical instructions, and has even declared himself in favour of this mode of thinking in general, with respect to all philosophical subjects. "Would not a well understood scepticism," says he among other things, "be the most natural way to a-
"void all metaphysical controversy, and at the same time the
"most rational means for calming all dogmatical and critical
"passions? What can be our aim under the titles of Logic,
"Metaphysics, Critic of Reason; what else can be our object
"under the general title of Philosophy than, after admitting
"the unquestionable reality of our representations, to sketch
"faithfully the history of them; and *then* to prove what
"is true and certain with respect to them; and what in the
"human mind (whether it be the lower, or more exalted part
"of it) carries the conviction of truth and certainty along
"with it?"—This philosopher wishes the whole of his work to be considered merely as the *subjective* conviction of a Sceptic, and describes the sceptical mode of thinking more accurately than has been done by any of his predecessors. In opposition to the Critique of Kant, he has started a number of questions, some of which are completely in the spirit of the old Pyrrhonists. —Upon these doubtful points, likewise, answers have already been published by the friends of the Critical System. However conclusive such refutations may appear to the party, on whose behalf they were attempted, it still remains to be wished, though there is now little hope left for this prospect, that the aged Father of Rational and Critical Dogmatism may deign to defend himself against the attacks of Plattner, and those of the New Aenesidemus.

With pleasure I proceed, by opposing to these sceptical writings a work written with noble intentions. Although it deviate in some respects from the principles of Kant, yet it supports, with energy, the truth and certainty of human knowledge,

knowledge, and at the same time places the interesting nature of these questions in a clear point of view.—The treatise, here alluded to, is " On Truth and moral perfection; by ADAM WEISHAUPT, 1793."

All the writings of Sceptics, it is sincerely to be hoped, will never totally deprive man of the belief in objective truth; and the Sceptic himself will never be capable of abandoning it completely. For it is of the utmost importance, that we should admit something objective, for the sake of morality and religion, both of which must lose their value, and their existence, as soon as they are considered merely as something subjective and relative. Philosophers ought, therefore, rather to justify the belief in objective reality, than represent to us, that there is no other but subjective conviction, which they hold out as the highest step of philosophical and consistent thought.—We cannot, indeed, proceed beyond the power of comprehension, and all conviction merely rests on our state of mind; but could it be otherwise?—It is sufficient that, in our consciousness, clear traces are given us of objective truth; that it is in our power to distinguish objective and subjective truth from one another; and that from the whole mode of our thought and action, and from the ideas of duty exalted above all necessity, we must reasonably admit *something objectively true*.

Philosophical Scepticism, which is not merely pretended, or affected, and which does not flow from an impure source, has as yet found, and ever will find, but a few *genuine* supporters: but when it is taught and extolled in writings, and in public places of instruction, it may, in a great number of individuals, gradually produce a shallow mode of sceptical reasoning, destroy the spirit of inquiry, and ultimately promote immorality. Perhaps, Philosophy would soon fall into disrepute, and the public spirit among mankind, as well as the general utility of the learned, would suffer extremely, were our attention confined

fined merely to the description of the phenomena that occur in the mind, and to the limited consideration of what is subjective alone, without placing any value upon what is objective.—It would be rash and irrational, to obtrude our maxims, opinions, and convictions upon others; though every one wishes to cultivate what *alone* is stable in us, our *reason*; and to try by gentle and suitable means, to bring to the clear consciousness and conviction of others, what our fair and candid examination teaches us to be uniformly true and good. We wish not, individually, to consider ourselves as insulated creatures that live, each of us, in our own world of ideas; but to believe, that we all have a claim upon a certain number of truths, and that it depends upon our own exertions, to get possession of these.

In our times, it might be more dangerous than many imagine, to represent the Scepticism of Hume as incontrovertible, or incapable of solution; for the greater number of superficial readers might thus be induced to surrender their weak minds to the most dangerous apathy, to shun every mental exertion, to search for no further discoveries in the department of philosophy, and—by gradually returning to the age of barbarism—to leave every thing in this deplorable situation, in which they themselves ultimately fall victims to infidelity, or fanaticism.

There prevails at present, in almost every civilized country, a very shallow and dangerous scepticism, extending its influence over the most important objects. It has assumed a systematic form, to which people readily subscribe; because it is more discreet, and less intolerable, than the *professed* mode of thinking, which characterizes almost every philosophic sect. This species of scepticism, in the greater number of individuals, assumes the appearance of an indolent and irresolute disposition of mind; and in many, that of a wild, fanatical fickleness; a fickleness, with which one party, by way of retaliation, usually reproaches the other.

The causes of this singular propensity, it is not difficult to trace: an inclination for sensual indulgence is every where manifest; the interest in *pure intellectual truth* is universally weakened; the old philosophical and theological systems have been shaken in their foundations, while the new ones have as yet been able to procure but little public reputation.

Prof. STÆUDLIN distinguishes with accuracy the different species of scepticism, and he endeavours to ascertain their true origin.—As a specimen of his masterly method of inquiry, I conclude this *Introduction*, with a faithful extract from his Treatise " On the Sources and Origin of Scepticism."

" There is," says he, " a certain kind of scepticism which deserves to be stiled the *philosophical*, and which arises nearly in the following manner. Men of vigorous minds, in whom a lively interest for every important truth is joined to an uncommon degree of penetration and activity, begin to think, and to inquire for themselves: such men divest themselves of their juvenile opinions and prejudices, at a much earlier period of life, than others. Their propensity to peculiar and original ideas exhibits every thing in a suspicious light, which formerly, either from mere custom or authority, had formed a part of their creed. The constant desire of discovering truth; the strong consciousness of their own powers to search for it; the bold prospect of opening, perhaps, new views in philosophy, continually induce them to inquire into every source, from which truth may be derived:—thus they are impelled by a kind of philosophic enthusiasm."

" That remarkable epoch of human life, in which sometimes the painter, sometimes the poet, as if by inspiration, feels in himself the genius of his art; this epocha has been frequently observed by men whom nature had designed for celebrity,

lebrity. The philosophic genius, not unfrequently, discovers a similar period, in which the views he directs to his intellectual nature, the manner in which he reflects upon the whole created fabric, and the researches he makes into the writings of the ancient philosophers, fill his mind with a pleasing anxiety, with a lively energy, and lead him to augur his future destiny: but this exertion of evolving talents not rarely terminates in scepticism. His mind trespasses upon regions unknown, and far remote from human conception; he is first induced, and that most frequently, to start questions which, to men, are altogether unanswerable. Unfortunately, too, he begins with the most difficult subjects of inquiry; for the more easy propositions appear to him beneath his dignity. The latter he treats with contempt; and grasping principally at the former, he is continually disappointed by the transient hopes of discovering mysteries, which lie concealed behind an impenetrable gloom. The unsuccessful efforts made upon that which is difficult, soon render him suspicious of what is both easy, and within his horizon. He wanders from one system to another in order to find the philosopher's stone; (or, as it is very forcibly expressed in the original) *to solve the riddle of the world*. He alternately pays homage to the different systems, which engage his attention; so that at one time the adherents of LOCKE, at another those of LEIBNITZ, at another those of DESCARTES, and at length those of ROUSSEAU are, with him, the representatives of truth. Sometimes, he creates systems of his own; but they are as quickly destroyed, as they were erected."

" He is, finally, led to investigate the foundation of all human knowledge and evidence, as well as to inquire into the possibility of an *objective* truth. Here, where he was in search of a certain resting point, a boisterous ocean of uncertainties, at once, appears in view. In vain he attempts, after the most accurate scrutiny of his intellectual powers, to discover the general and necessary characters of truth. His sensations, every where, appear to inform him of things, not in unison with his reason; and upon the most important concerns, which inspire his heart with hopes and desires, his reason is silent; or it torments him with such doubts and apprehensions, as are sufficient to blast his most sanguine expectations. In vain he endeavours to reconcile that at least, in which the opinions of all men coincide, with the general characters of truth. With indignation he observes the contradictory opinions of the greatest philosophers of all ages; with surprise he sees, how frequently he had already imagined himself in the possession of truth; and how frequently he had also been obliged to reject it, as illusory. The most opposite judgments of men, even in common life; the operation of physical causes; the influence of the passions, of authority, and of the most incidental circumstances, as affecting these judgments,—now excite the whole of his attention. The observation, that innumerable multitudes had from the beginning of time lived happy, and found the most complete conviction in speculative fancies and errors; this observation makes him despair of discovering certainty in any subject whatever. With a compassionate smile he beholds the dogmatist, bold and decisive, proud and self-sufficient, proposing his opinions, in which he discovers little more, than proofs of ignorance, or of arrogance and dissimulation. At last, he forms the resolution of renouncing all discoveries tending to establish absolute truth; of deducing in every instance no other than doubtful results; and of obtruding his judgments as little upon any man, as he would be inclined to adopt them from others. But as he feels in himself an irresistible propensity, still to adopt *some* things, and to lay down for himself some rules of conduct, not being able to act altogether without

out *fixed* principles; there is no wonder that he bestows his approbation upon some sentiments and judgments; yet he does this with the constant restriction, *that these are by no means absolute, and that they are true only as to himself.*"

" The philosophical scepticism, the origin and progress of which we have here described, is, however, extremely rare. We meet more frequently, particularly in the present age, with other species of it, which arise from very different sources, and which may with more justice be termed *premeditated pyrrhonism,* or a decided propensity of the mind to universal doubt."

" Scepticism, also, frequently derives its origin from indolence and ignorance. Some people acquire a superficial knowledge of the history of philosophical opinions; they are perhaps informed, that there has been a set of men who doubted every thing; they are fond of claiming the name of philosophers, who are not blind followers of others, and who rise above the common set of men. Instead of instituting profound inquiries into the nature of the human faculties for acquiring knowledge; instead of calmly and patiently comparing the opinions of philosophers; they raise a host of doubts upon every subject, that requires acute reflection: thus they study the art of contriving endless objections."

" It is, indeed, much easier and more convenient to frame objections against every conclusion, than to draw the result from laborious researches, and to defend this result against the objections of others.*—When a subject is only in part understood, doubts must spontaneously arise, which may confound the

---

* BAYLE, in his letter to MINUTELLI; " *Oeuvres div. IV.* p. 537." very justly remarks: " En verité, il ne faut pas trouver etrange, que tant de gens
" aient donné dans le Pyrrhonisme: car c'est la chose du monde la plus commode.
" Vous pouvez impunement disputer contre tous venans, et sans craindre ces
" argumens ad hominem, qui font quelque-fois tant de peine. Vous craignez
" point la retorsion; puisque ne soutenant rien vous abandonnez de bon coeur a
" tous

the clearest proposition. Among this class of ignorant and shallow sceptics, we frequently meet with the strangest compounds of scepticism, credulity and dogmatism. They are apt to believe the grossest absurdities, provided that the objects be very contiguous to their sight, and require no acute investigation: but they entertain doubts concerning the demonstrative evidence of mathematics, and the reality of moral law."

" Ambition, a fondness for paradoxes and novelty, are, with many, the principal springs of scepticism. It is something so very uncommon to doubt every thing; it discovers so much boldness, superiority, acuteness and liberality, so much art, to combat every opinion that enters into the common creed. On the other hand, it appears so very modest, when in imitation of SOCRATES—the sceptical genius pretends to know nothing; nay, he goes even farther, in confessing, that he is not quite certain of *this!* Such is his modesty, produced by a still greater impulse of self-denial."

> Nil sciri quisquis putat, id quoque nescit
> An sciri possit quo se nil scire fatetur.
>
> LUCRET. IV. 471.

" It is a peculiar satisfaction, to triumph over that pedantic dogmatism, which arises sometimes from ignorance, sometimes from an abundance of *knowing*, but not of *real knowledge*. It is a pleasing reflection, to behold the ardent contest of opinions, and to look on this dangerous and tempestuous passage upon the sea of human uncertainties, with a calm, perhaps affected, resignation."

> Suave mari magno turbantibus æquora ventis
> E terra magnum alterius spectare laborem,
> Non quia vexari quemquam, est jucunda voluptas,
> Sed quibus ipse malis careas, quia cernere suave est.

" We

" tous les sophismes et a tous les raisonnemens de la terre quelque opinion que ce
" soit. En un mot vous contestez et vous *daubez* sur toutes choses tout votre
" saoul, sans craindre de peine du talion."

"We find, in the records of philosophical history, many celebrated characters who were professed sceptics, and who, in that history still shine as luminaries: though, by the moderns, consigned to obscurity. Is it not honourable, to rank among men of such celebrity?—This ambitious scepticism, certainly, arises from immoral sources: it is productive of frequent mischief, both in the moral character of those who profess it, and of those who listen to this deception. Its progress, in the present age, is very considerable.—As the modern system of toleration is frequently the most intolerant, this modern scepticism also frequently appears in the highest degree fanatical and magisterial. By means of this delusive art, men *of a certain description* endeavour to render *every thing* doubtful, which is believed by the generality of mankind; to destroy without mercy, all the antiquated forms and species of belief, and to impose upon us the inventions of their own brain, in the most insinuating and decisive tone. Unhappily, they find easy access, through the vices and passions of man, so that great moral and political revolutions have been frequently produced, in consequence of metaphysical speculations which, at first, seemed to have little, or no influence, upon the practice of life."

" Avoid those—says the Vicar of Savoy to the young man, to whom he delivers his confession of faith—" who, under
" the pretext of expounding nature, fill the heart of men with
" inert doctrines, and whose apparent scepticism is infinitely
" more decisive and dogmatical, than the positive tone of their
" adversaries. Under the ambitious pretence, that they alone
" are enlightened, veracious and sincere, they imperiously
" subject us to their destructive decisions, while they affect
" to communicate to us the true principles of things, by
" means of those unintelligible systems which are the produc-
" tions of their own fancy. Hence, they subvert, destroy, and
" trample

"trample under foot, every thing that is venerable to man
"in society; they deprive the afflicted of the last comfort in
"their calamities; the rich and powerful of the only bridle
"of their passions; they snatch the stings of conscience from
"the recesses of the heart; their propitious hopes from the
"virtuous; and withal, they still boast of having been the
"benefactors of the human race. Never, they say, is truth
"pernicious to man. I believe this, as well as they; but
"this very circumstance is, in my opinion, a strong proof,
"that *their* doctrines cannot claim the character of truth."

Luxury and degeneracy of manners are perfectly consistent, as well with each other, as with a partial illumination and improvement of the mind. If we neglect to unfold the mental faculties; if the interest which ties us to the intellectual and invisible (not, visionary) world gradually vanishes; then this immoral and shallow scepticism easily arises, and infects even numerous classes of society. It carries along with it the appearance of cultivation and enlargement of mind; but, at the same time, it opens an extensive field to every selfish desire.

Legion is the number of the deluded, who are in search of illumination of mind, chiefly by disputing and cavilling upon close subjects of intellectual inquiry, which were formerly held to be most true and worthy of veneration. Those fortunate travellers, whose object, in visiting the reputed Capitals of Europe, was not amusement alone; they must have the clearest proofs, how much that flimsy mode of reasoning now prevails, and how certain it is, that it arises from the sources here mentioned. The authors of the most enlightened nations of Europe agree that, many new philosophical productions, as they are called, are nothing but the offspring of this crude and unphilosophical scepticism.*

Many

* Vid. for instance "Letters of Literature, by Robert Heron; London, 1785."—a strang medley of undigested thoughts.

HISTORICAL INTRODUCTION.

Many remarkable events of the present age may be considered as the consequences of a philosophy—without having the least claim to that dignified name—which undermines the pillars of every useful institution, but rears no fabric; which leaves man in a state of indolence and indifference with respect to his most important concerns; and which converts him into a sensual and selfish being, that is determined solely by time, accident, and circumstances; and that is tossed, to and fro, on this sea of life, without a rudder or compass, without a sure rule for his conduct or belief, without any fixed object, to which his future prospects and hopes can be rationally directed.

> Placed on this isthmus of a middle state,
> A being darkly wise and rudely great:
> With too much knowledge for the sceptic side,
> With too much weakness for the Stoics pride,
> He hangs between; in doubt to act, or rest;
> In doubt to deem himself a God or beast;
> In doubt, his mind or body to prefer;
> Born but to die, and reas'ning but to err;
> Alike in ignorance, his reason such,
> Whether he thinks too little, or too much:
> Chaos of thought and passion, all confus'd,
> Still by himself abus'd, or disabus'd;
> Created half to rise, and half to fall;
> Great lord of all things, yet a prey to all;
> Sole judge of truth, in endless error hurl'd:
> The glory, jest, and riddle of the world.
>   POPE.

ELEMENTARY VIEW

OF THE

PHILOSOPHY OF KANT.

Preparatory Remarks.

BEFORE we enter upon this arduous task, it may be of some importance to premise a few necessary observations on the method which has been adopted in the execution of it; and on the various obstacles which the student of every new System, particularly of Ethics, must unavoidably encounter.

It appeared to me, at a very early period of my studies, that the principal dissensions, and subsequent divisions in philosophy, have arisen *chiefly* from the following obvious sources. —Every systematic writer on subjects, which, from their nature, do not admit of demonstrative certainty, nor of any such proofs as are manifest from *objective reality*, is almost involuntarily led to employ new terms and phrases, in order to express the different opinions he broaches among his cotemporaries. It is of little consequence *to him*, whether the ideas, which gave rise to these opinions, be also new. For, though the latter may be already germinating in the seeds sown by his great predecessors, or may only have been differently explained, he is equally certain of finding *some* adherents, who pride themselves upon discovering a new sense, or perhaps a new application of the sense, in which his terms, the definitions of them, or the scientific divisions, are now more clearly, or more obscurely, understood. This has uniformly happened, I could

almost

almost say, since the beginning of philosophical speculations: hence the absolute necessity of giving, in every instance, the clearest possible definitions of words, must be obvious to every novice in philosophy. But this I consider as a task, the *strict* performance of which, from the very imperfect state of language, has been (and probably will never cease to be) one of the many *human desiderata*. Hence, the immortal BACON, when the same, or at least a similar idea pervaded his comprehensive mind, was induced to express himself upon this subject, in the following excellent words: " *Præterea ut bene sperent, Instaurationem nostram ut quiddam infinitum et ultra mortale fingant, et animo concipiant; cum revera fit infiniti erroris finis et terminus legitimus.*"

Were it, however, possible to define *all* philosophical terms with that degree of precision which we, sometimes, observe in the works of a BACON, a NEWTON, and a KANT; yet we could also suggest the remark—a remark which is by no means in favour of human perfection—that even these illustrious characters, in their own elementary works, not rarely deviate from the original, or primary, definitions of terms. Those, who are conversant in speculative inquiries, will readily, and within proper limits, understand this assertion; and such readers as might extend the meaning of it further than I am inclined to admit, I only remind of the *logical* difficulties attending every long demonstration. It would, therefore, be rash in the extreme to charge these eminent characters with incongruity of thought, or reasoning; as the *more minute* deviations, *in terms*, are chiefly owing to the unsettled state of language in general; and as the very term, *perfection*, when speaking of human beings provided with human organs, is only *relative*.

A long and dear-bought experience in teaching has first induced me to entertain thoughts upon this important theme, which may not find many supporters. Yet I think myself justified in asserting, that the most, if not all, Systems of Grammar and Rhetoric, as well as the Dictionaries of languages, are compiled upon mechanical, wavering and untenable principles;* for they are, more or less, liable to the following serious objections:

1st. That the rules contained in Grammars, generally admit of a greater number of *exceptions*, than of *positive determinations*.

2d. That the inflections of nouns and verbs are not accommodated to the *etymology* of words, but are chiefly taken from *analogy*;—a circumstance productive of endless mistakes and confusion in the grammars of *modern* languages.

3d. That so far from improving the phrases and idioms of languages, grammarians seem to labour hard to render them, if possible, more perplexed and inconsistent; †—by daily adopting new idioms in one language, which are borrowed from another; by using words in a figurative *sense*, which cannot be *thus* employed without impropriety; by transferring words from the *physical* to the moral *sense*, and vice versa, when there is no other necessity for this outrage upon *good sense*

---

* Whether the *Elementary Grammar* of the *German* Language, which I propose to publish, together with an *Identical Dictionary* of the *German*, *English*, *French* and *Latin* languages, will be liable to the charges which my predecessors have incurred, I am not confident enough to aver. The short specimen given of the latter at the end of this work) which accompanies the third: "Essay, On the merits and demerits of JOHNSON's English Dictionary, on language in general, &c. by ADELUNG," will serve as a tolerable criterion of the execution of the whole.

† If it be objected, that this is no fault of Grammarians, since language is formed and modelled by a whole people, I shall briefly answer; that tradition and custom *alone* do not appear to have any such tendency, as to make a whole nation speak and write jargon, or nonsense, for ever; and consequently, that errors and mistakes ought not to be perpetuated in *elementary* books of instruction.

sense, than the fancy or caprice of the speaker, and subsequently, that of the writer *.

4th. That instead of giving a syntax of speech, or sentences arranged in the most natural order, and still conformable to the premises, as well as to the subsequent conclusions, they adhere to the opposite extreme; by neglecting the *general*, and giving the *special* construction of the individual parts.— This, indeed, is of itself a useful piece of labour, if the rules were not too much crowded upon the tyro; but it by no means deserves the name of a *syntax*, for its object is merely the *inflection* of nouns and verbs, as preparatory to a *General Syntax* †.

5th. That no Grammarian, or Lexicographer, excepting perhaps ADELUNG, has accurately and *uniformly* distinguished, both the *moral* and *physical* sense of words—however easy this may appear at first sight—nor the *objective* and *subjective* application of terms and phrases ‡.

As

---

* This charge cannot, in justice, be levelled at the captivating effusions of Poetry; an art which, from its nature, and the frequent good effects it produces in rousing, like music, the palsied organs of mortals, deserves more deference, than any of the liberal arts; as it is likewise understood to possess a much greater latitude, than all the sister-arts.

† Upon accurate investigation, it must strike even the novice in grammar, that there can be only *two parts* in the nature of speech, which being the *regulators* of all the Data involved in the rest, produce that change of place, or situation, which we express by the term *Syntax*: these *two* unquestionably, are the nominative of the *Noun*, with its corresponding *Verb*.—All other parts of speech are, in my opinion, liable to the same modifications, or changes, which characterize a numerous progeny, whose father and mother alone are stable and fixed.

‡ The immortal author of the " Critique of Pure Reason" was, among the Germans, without exception the first, who perceived the *absolute* necessity of this distinction in philosophical inquiries.—In justice to the high rank held by the English and French philosophers, however, I must frankly own, (what I have, in part, already declared in the Preface) that I have not been so happily situated as to examine, with critical accuracy, *their* respective *nomenclatures*. But if I may

rely

As KANT's *Critique of Pure Reason* is the principal elementary work, upon the pillars of which the whole of his System, together with all the works that illustrate it, must either stand, or fall, we shall first explain its *aim* and *moral tendency*, by giving KANT's peculiar definition and division of philosophy, accompanied with *five connected problems*; and in the next place, it will be useful to lay down the *particular contents* of *all* his works. The former we shall exhibit in the *Synopsis*:* the latter must be the feeble effort of a *literal*, not elegant, translation; and we propose to comprise them in the subsequent *Chronological Analysis*.

I. SYNOPSIS.

A. DEFINITION AND DIVISION OF PHILOSOPHY.

Philosophy is the system of all philosophical, i. e. *discursive* knowledge derived from bare ideas, or notions.—This is the scholastic definition; but, in a cosmological sense, it is the science concerning the relation of all our knowledge to the essential purposes of human reason, (teleologia rationis humanæ) and the philosopher is not an architect of reason, but the

---

rely upon the information of that learned and sagacious pupil, who condescended to translate the *Synoptical Problems* here stated, with their solutions, as a specimen of his progress in the German.——Dr REID, of Glasgow, was the first among the British Philosophers, who distinguished clearly between the *objective* and *subjective* use of the words, which are employed to express the immediate objects of *sensation* and *perception*.

* Originally digested by Mr JOHN SCHULZE, an eminent Divine and Court-Chaplain at Koenigsberg; a particular friend of KANT's who, on that occasion, congratulated him upon having *fully* entered into the spirit of the CRITIQUE; and bestowed upon him every mark of approbation.

the law-giver of it. We cannot, hence, learn philosophy itself; it is philosophizing which ought to be our study.

---

1. *Philosophical Knowledge*
    a.) is *discursive*, as derived from ideas, and opposed to mathematical *intuitive* knowledge, derived from the construction of ideas.
    b.) is to be understood *objectively*:
        1.—as the prototype for judging upon all the attempts of philosophizing.
        2.—as a bare idea of a possible science, which is no where given *in concreto*: for where is it? who is in the possession of it? and by what means may it be distinguished from others?
    c.) considers particulars only in the general; while mathematical knowledge considers general subjects in the particular, nay, even in the individual.—Those who pretend, that *quality* is the object of philosophy, *quantity* the object of mathematics, have erroneously adopted the effect, instead of the cause.
2. The *scholastic definition of philosophy* denotes a system of knowledge, which we pursue only with a view of reducing it to scientific rules, without any other aim, than that of attaining to a logical perfection of knowledge.—Thus philosophy is merely considered as one of those arts, which may be applied to certain arbitrary purposes; and in this sense the philosopher is an architect of reason.
3. The *cosmological idea of philosophy* implies that, which necessarily concerns every individual.—In this view the philosopher is the legislator of human reason.
4. *Among the essential purposes of human reason*, one is the

final

final purpose, and this is the *complete* destination of man. The philosophy which has this purpose for its object, is called Ethics. Hence the ancients always understood by the name philosopher, at the same time, and principally, the Moralist, the Stoic, or him who can govern himself.

5. To *Philosophize*, means to exercise, by certain plain experiments, the talent which reason displays in judging conformably to its general principles.—According to Kant's System, philosophy is divided into, and considered as

1st. *formal* (methodical) *philosophy*, which concerns merely the form of the understanding and reasoning faculties, as well as the general rules of thought, throughout independent of the objects: hence *Logic*, *Canon* for understanding and reasoning.

2d. *material philosophy*, such as is employed in reflecting upon any one object, and again is

A. the *pure*, or the philosophy of pure reason, which depends upon fundamental principles and notions *a priori*. This is,

    a. *Propædeutic*, or *Critique*, which inquires into the faculty of reason with respect to all its pure knowledge a priori;

    b. *Metaphysics in a more extensive sense*, the system of pure reason; or the collective philosophical knowledge from pure reason, in systematic connection, whether real, or imaginary.—This again comprehends

        a.) *Metaphysics of Nature*; Metaphysics in a more limited sense, that of the speculative use of pure reason, which confines its inquiries to what actually is, or exists. Its component parts are the following four:

           aa. *Ontology*, the system of all ideas and princi-
ples

ples, which relate to subjects in general, without proposing any objects of perception.

bb. *Rational Physiology*, which investigates nature, i. e. the complexus (compass) of subjects; whether they be exhibited to the senses, or to any other perceptive faculty. It comprepends 1st, *Rational* (not empirical) *Physics*, treating of material objects, and including every thing that may be known by means of the external senses;—2d, *Rational Psychology*, which considers the subject of the internal sense, mind; and, according to its fundamental notions, the reflecting capacity in general.

cc. *Rational Cosmology*, which employs itself with the internal combination of the objects of experience; but which proceeds beyond the possibility of experience; *general knowledge of the world*, by which nature is considered as an absolute Universum.

dd. *Rational Theology*, which investigates the connection subsisting between Nature and a Supreme Being.

b.) *Metaphysics of Morals*, or the practical use of pure reason, which attends to the laws, according to which every thing happens in this, and no other, manner;—*pure morals, Ethics*.

B. The *experimental, practical Philosophy*, which is altogether established upon experience, and again consists of three principal divisions, viz.

1. *Physics*, the experimental doctrine of the material world.

2. *Psychology*, the experimental doctrine of mind.

3. *Anthropology*, the practical doctrine of free-acting man, derived from experience.

Corrolaria.

1. Material Philosophy is, therefore, divided like Mathematics, into *pure* and *applied* (practical).
2. There are, originally, only *two* principal divisions of philosophy, *Logic* and *Metaphysics*; or, according to the plan of the ancient Greeks, *three*; namely, *Logic, Physics*, and *Ethics*.

B. Problems and Solutions.

Exordium.

The aim of Kant's *Critique* is no less, than to lead Reason to the true knowledge of itself; to examine the titles, upon which it founds the supposed possession of its metaphysical knowledge, and by means of this examination to mark the true limits, beyond which it cannot venture to speculate, without wandering into the empty region of pure fancy;— an attempt, the bare idea of which sufficiently discovers the philosophic spirit of its author.

In order to acquire a correct notion of the term *Pure Reason*, we must consider it in this point of view.—Every act of judgment, which is not mingled with any *heterogeneous* ingredients, is called *pure*. But particularly every piece of comparative knowledge, which is unmixed with any experience, or sensation, and which consequently is possible altogether a priori, deserves the name of *absolutely pure*; v. g. *Liberty, God, Immortality*.—Reason, then, is that faculty, which affords to us the principles of comparative knowledge a priori.

Hence

Hence *pure reason* contains the principles of judging upon any thing *absolutely* a priori. The whole compass of those principles, conformably to which all pure judgments a priori can be acquired and carried into effect, might be called an *Organon* of pure reason.—The whole Critique of pure reason, therefore, is established upon this principle, (not *postulate*, nor *petitio principii*, but the result of an appeal to *acts of consciousness*) *that there is a free reason independent of all experience and sensation**.

Reason, as the organ of mind *in concreto*, must be considered, both subjectively, and objectively. *Subjective* reason is capable of perpetual increase, by approximation to the *objective* state of it, viz. to the perfect model, (standard).

Problem First.

To determine the nature of the Sensitive Faculty and its distinction from Understanding.

1. The *Sensitive Faculty* consists in the capacity of our Soul to receive immediate representations of objects, merely from being affected by them in this or that way.

2. The representations, which the Sensitive faculty affords to us, are therefore referred to the object which affects us, i. e. they are *Perceptions*.

---

* Although M. SELLE, one of KANT's opponents, has endeavoured to prove, in an Essay published in the *Berlin Monthly Magazine*, for December 1784, " *that there are no pure ideas of the reasoning faculty, independent of experience ;*" yet I think it necessary to remind the reader, that all such *negative proofs*, as arise from the *subjective* conviction of an individual, say as little against the validity, or stability, of a philosophical proposition which altogether depends on the manner of exhibiting it to the mind, as the failure of converting the Turks and Jews to the Christian Religion, can furnish any argument to the disadvantage of the latter.

3. All our Perceptions have a twofold form, *Space and Time*, as representations which relate to objects, and which are themselves Perceptions, pure Perceptions that, a priori, previous to all actual sensation, are discoverable originally in the representing capacity of our Soul, and lie already at the foundation of all our actual sensations, as necessary conditions of their possibility.

4. Hence Space and Time are not something attached to objects themselves, but mere subjective representations *in us*. The Being in Space and Time, consequently extension, impenetrability, succession, change, motion, &c. are therefore not qualities which belong to objects *in themselves*, but representations in our minds, which attach barely to the nature of our Sensitive Faculty. In other words, the motion of matter does not produce representations in us, but is itself mere representation.

5. Hence also we know things merely as they appear to us; that is, we know only the impressions which they make on *our* Sensitive Faculty; but what they may be in themselves, and for *other* reasonable Beings, is altogether unknown to us.

Problem Second.

To investigate the whole store of original notions discoverable in our Understanding, and which lie at the foundation of all our knowledge; and at the same time to authenticate their true descent, by showing that they are not derived from experience, but are pure productions of the understanding.

1. The perceptions of objects contain, indeed, the matter of knowledge, but are in themselves *blind* and *dead*, and not knowledge: and our soul is merely passive in regard to them.

2. If these perceptions are to furnish knowledge, the *Understanding* must think of them, and this is possible only through *notions* (conceptions), which are the peculiar Form of our Under-

Understanding, in the same manner, as Space and time are the Form of our Sensitive Faculty.

3. These notions are active representations of our understanding-faculty; and as they regard *immediately* the perceptions of objects, they refer to the objects themselves only mediately.

4. They lie in our Understanding, as pure notions a priori, at the foundation of all our knowledge: they are necessary forms, radical notions, Categories, (Predicaments) of which all our knowledge must be compounded: and the Table of them follows.

Quantity: Unity, Plurality, Totality.
Quality: Reality, Negation, Limitation.
Relation: Substance, Cause, Reciprocation.
Modality: Possibility, Existence, Necessity.

5. Now to *think* and to *judge* is the same thing; consequently every notion contains a particular form of judgment concerning objects. There are *four* principal *genera* of *judgments*: they are derived from the above four possible functions of the Understanding, each of which contains under it *three species*, namely with respect to

Quantity, they are universal, particular, singular
Quality, ———— affirmative, negative, infinite
Relation, ———— cathegorical, hypothetical, disjunctive
Modality, ———— problematical, assertory, apodictical

} Judgments.

6. And thus not only the whole power of our understanding is fathomed out of its own nature, and therefore perfectly a priori; but also, at the same time, the pure descent of our notions from the Understanding; and their perfect independence on all experience, is proved.

Problem Third.

To shew in what manner we are entitled to ascribe objective reality

reality to those notions, which are merely something subjective in us; or in other words, to shew how the understanding is justified in going, as it were, out of itself, and in transferring its notions to things which are external to it, that is, to refer them to objects.

1. Space and time are, as pure perceptions a priori, merely *subjective*; but as *forms* of our *Sensitive Faculty*, they have a necessary relation to objects of sense,—are necessary Predicates of whatever can be an object of sensation; and therefore the following synthetical principles a priori are established:

a. Every thing that can be an object of our external senses, so as to be perceived or felt, is in *Space*; and all the predicates of space, extension, divisibility, &c. *necessarily* belong to it.

b. Every thing that can be an object of our senses in general, whether external or internal, is in *Time*; and therefore, all the predicates of time, simultaneity, succession, &c. also *of necessity* belong to it.

2. In like manner, all pure notions a priori are, indeed, something merely *subjective* in our Understanding; but as *forms* of our *Thought* (of the Thinking Faculty), they must likewise relate to all objects of our Sensitive Faculty. Hence the following universal synthetical maxim, a priori, is established.

Every thing which can be an object of possible experience, must not only be in Space and Time; but to it also must belong *one* of each class of the pure notions of the understanding.

3. Our notions, therefore, receive relation to objects, or *objective reality*, only through a third mediating representation a priori, which has something in common with the perception, as well as with the notion, and by means of which, therefore, the union of the Notion with the Object becomes possible.

possible. This, in reality, is *Time*, which KANT calls the Schema of Notions*; for it has something common with all

per-

---

* The *Schemata* are *indetermined sensualized representations which the imagination places under pure notions of the Understanding*; and conformably to the Number of the Categories, they may be exhibited in the following Table:

1. QUANTITY, i. e. Series of time.
    Number.
2. QUALITY, i. e. things contained in time.
    Reality, i. e. existence, sensation in time, time filled.
    Negation, i. e. non-existence, absence of feeling, vacuum in time.
    Limitation, i. e. transition from feeling through its various degrees, till it has vanished, or vice versa.
3. RELATION, i. e. arrangement in time, relation of feelings to each other in time.
    Substantiality, i. e. the real, in so far as it is permanent in, and with, time—the substratum of all changes: and accidents, i. e. the real in so far as it changes.
    Casuality, i. e. succession of different feelings in time, conformably to a rule.
    Community, i. e. simultaneity of feeling, according to rule.
4. MODALITY, i. e. the modes, in which an object belongs to time.
    Possibility, i. e. the representation of a thing, conformably to the conditions of any one time in general.
    Actuality, i. e. the representation of a thing, in a determinate time.
    Necessity, i. e. the representation of a thing at all times.

(FINIS)

perceptions, because it is itself a perception a priori, and it has something common with all notions a priori; because it is a Form of all Sensations and Representations a priori. The uniting of a pure Notion with an object is, therefore, possible merely through time as its Schema.

4. Through means of this Schema, according to the Table given in the preceeding note, all synthetical axioms may now be exactly determined a priori, and they are the following:

Axiom of Quantity, (or of perception). " All phenomena in perception are exhibited under the notion of extension."

Axiom of Quality, (or of the anticipation of observation). " In all phenomena, sensation, and the reality which corresponds to it in the object, have *intensive quantum*, or a degree; that is, every reality can, through infinite gradations, become less and less, till it be $= 0$."

Axioms of Relation, (or Analogies of experience).

    a. " In all phenomena there is something permanent, i. e. Substance; and something shifting, or accidents."

    b. Every event has a cause.

    c. All substances, so far as they are co-existent, stand in reciprocation with each other.

Axioms of Modality, (or Postulates).

    a. That which agrees with the form of experience (according to Perception and Notion) is possible really, not merely logically.

    b. That which is connected with the matter of experience, i. e. with sensation, is actual.

    c. That which is connected with what is actual, agreeably to the universal conditions of experience, is (exists) necessary.

Problem Fourth.

To determine by these means the true bounds of human reason, consequently to explain positively, how far our reason can reach through mere speculation, where; on the contrary, our proper knowledge ceases, and nothing but faith and hope remain.

1. All the elementary notions, of which our Understanding is capable, are exactly those which the foregoing Table of them indicates, so that there are neither more nor less of them in number.

2. All these elementary notions are applicable merely to sensible objects, and hence they serve only for determining the necessary predicates of every possible perception. From this the following consequences result.

    a. We cannot apply our notions to the most perfect Being; consequently we cannot prove that he has extension, or qualities; that he is a substance, a cause of other things; that he is possible or actual, or necessary.

    b. Even as to the objects of our sensitive faculty, all our elementary notions can teach us none of the predicates that belong to them in themselves, that is, to their Essence; but all predicates which, through these notions, can be ascribed to them, concern merely their perception, and the union of the varieties in it, consequently the way merely, in which they *appear* to us. Things in respect of what they are in themselves, are no objects, either of our senses or of our understanding.

    c. Hence the three *cosmological* questions are mere chimeras, viz.

        Whether the world, in point of space, be finite or infinite?

        Whether it has had a beginning, or has existed from eternity?

Whether the number of parts, of which matter consists, be finite or infinite?

d. But as the understanding cannot assert, or prove, any thing of objects that come not under the cognizance of the senses, as little can it deny, or refute them, by any argument that has even the appearance of validity. And hence arises the (sublime) presupposition and belief of a Supreme Being, and of an immortality of the Soul; because there are certain necessary purposes of human nature, moral laws, which require this presupposition.

e. Yet though we have sufficient *subjective* grounds for presupposing and determining certain supersensible objects; we have not, through such grounds, the least knowledge, how these objects may be constituted in themselves; but we try to determine them, only by analogy.

3. All the Synthetical Axioms of our Understanding, by means of which we are able to judge of objects, are *exactly* those which the foregoing Table of them indicates, and we know, therefore, a priori, the whole foundation of all the knowledge of which our Understanding is capable.

4. But all these axioms of our Understanding have objective validity, only so far as the possibility of experience depends on them; and they serve merely to determine the necessary connection of sensible things with each other. It may hence be justly said, that our Understanding, instead of first learning its axioms from nature, rather through them, a priori, prescribes laws to nature; and that on this account it is the *true legislature of nature,* so that, without these axioms of our Understanding, all regularity and order among the objects of sense, consequently the possibility of experience itself, would cease. Hence, too, as soon as we wish to rise with the axioms of our Understanding to supersensible objects beyond nature, we always make an unjustifiable use of them.

5. And as our *Understanding* can neither form a notion of supersensible objects, nor judge of them; as little can our *Reason* discover by inference any supersensible object; consequently, no Syllogism can lead us to new objects, which lie without the sphere of possible experience.

6. All notions which our reason can form of something, that is absolutely *unconditionate*, are therefore mere *Ideas*, whose objective validity can be proved through no species of Syllogism.

7. Hence the Axiom, " If the conditionate thing be given, the absolutely unconditionate thing is also given," is nothing but a subjective logical Maxim of Reason, i. e. a Maxim which regulates the train of reasoning in the Mind itself.

8. As now the whole of speculative Cosmology, Psychology and Theology entirely rests on this Axiom; these three Sciences, as far as concerns their speculative parts, are nothing but Systems of fallacies *. Ontology, also, completely fails, and must be changed into a bare Analysis of the notions of our Understanding.—The whole body of Metaphysics, then, must be confined to the Metaphysics of Nature.

PROBLEM FIFTH.

To solve the riddle, why our Reason is so irresistibly inclined to venture with its speculations beyond the bounds of possible knowledge;

---

* From what is here said, the reader may be led to suppose, that KANT altogether denies the possibility of proving the existence of a Supreme Being, the immortality of the Soul, &c. This supposition, however, would be ill-founded; for Kant distinctly and repeatedly admits the existence of these supersensible objects; but maintains, that we arrive at the knowledge of them through a process of practical, not speculative, Reason. This process he endeavours to vindicate and illustrate, by the most appropriate examples, in his *Critique of Practical Reason*, the contents of which the Reader will find in our CHRONOLOGICAL ANALYSIS.

knowledge; and hence to detect the fallacy, by which it is in this respect involuntarily deceived.

1. The ground of this irresistible bias lies in the nature of of our Reason itself. Reason cannot be satisfied with the original Notions and Axioms of the Understanding alone; but through categorical, hypothetical and disjunctive conclusions, it attains to the *Idea* of a simple substance, of an absolute Universum, of an absolute existent perfection in the number of real parts of matter, of an absolute perfection in the series of causes, of an absolute necessary Being, and of a Substance that possesses all realities.

2. Consequently the Idea of the absolutely unconditionate thing has indeed perfect *subjective* validity, and is in no manner an arbitrary fiction: Reason forces it on us necessarily. But hence it does not follow, that this Idea has also *objective* validity. Reason commits a very concealed, indeed, but undeniable sophism, when from mere Notions it forms the synthetical Axiom, " that, if the conditionate thing be given, so must be also the absolutely unconditionate."

3. As the Idea of absolutely unconditionate objects is indispensibly required by our Reason, it is very natural, that even the acutest philosopher should not only feel in himself an unavoidable bias to such fallacious conclusions; but also, that it must be very difficult for him to disencumber himself from them completely, though he be fortunate enough to discover the deception.

Scholion.

Thus, through the CRITIQUE of KANT, all these five problems, concerning the possibility and the limits of pure rational discoveries, have been thoroughly solved, but in a way which perhaps no philosopher had supposed. According to the result of this *Critique*, the possibility of pure rational knowledge, such as Metaphysics *can* furnish, *has been* established. But that knowledge extends no further, than to the world of sense, consequently only to the universal and necessary laws of nature. A demonstrably certain System of Metaphysics is indeed possible, but a very different one from what we have had hitherto, which, as its name indicates, sets out with propositions for judging dogmatically upon things discoverable beyond the region of Physics, i. e. without the limits of Nature.——If the principles above delineated be just, the *only possible* Metaphysics, so far as we are entitled to proceed dogmatically, are the *Metaphysics of Nature*.—Consequently the Critique of Kant considers all the Metaphysical Systems, which have been hitherto proposed, as false ware, and maintains that we have as yet no just Metaphysics. His own work is important and profound, and deserves to be carefully examined by those who are conversant in such studies. Whatever the result of this examination may be, philosophy will undoubtedly gain by it: and although the Critique of Kant should not stand the test of future, perhaps more successful researches, it will nevertheless form a remarkable epoch in the history of Metaphysical Science.

II. CHRONOLOGICAL ANALYSIS.

Exordium.

In venturing upon this essential part of the Elements, which are designed to afford a concise, though comprehensive view of the diversified labours of KANT, I deem it a duty incumbent upon me to state that, both his systematic works [*], as well as

those

---

[*] That these may be more easily distinguished from others, I have arranged them by a second number enclosed in ( ).

those which treat upon general subjects of philosophy, are here *successively* submitted to the consideration of the reader.

I must however remark that, consistent with the plan and extent of these *Elements*, the review of so great a variety of subjects cannot abound in Criticism; but I hope it will be found the more complete in the *analytical* part of it, comprehending *every* subject * treated by the illustrious author, during a period now exceeding half a century.

Though my abilities—the limited compass of which is best known to myself—were adequate to do the works of KANT that justice in reviewing them critically, to which they are certainly entitled; I would still hesitate to engage upon an undertaking, obviously not the most grateful, and in my relative situation, as a former pupil to the most renowned Professor in Europe, perhaps unbecoming. Hence I shall content myself with the humble province of briefly commenting upon the aim of every individual publication, and then of exhibiting the contents of each through a precise translation.

The difficulty of understanding the peculiar terms and expressions of KANT must, I have reason to hope, in great measure vanish; if the reader, in every instance, with patient and diligent application, resorts to the *Glossary*.

In order to characterize the early genius of the author, who, in the twenty-second year of his age, published an Essay upon one of the most abstruse subjects of inquiry, I shall conclude these preliminaries with the singular *Motto* prefixed to this juvenile production:

Nihil

---

* Those Essays, which have not been separately printed, and the most of which were published in the *Monthly Magazine of Berlin*, I could not procure from Germany; but I have still introduced them in this review, merely for the sake of completeness, upon the authority of *Prof.* WILL of *Altdorf*, and *Prof.* SCHMID of *Jena*.

Nihil magis præstandum est, quam ne pecorum ritu sequamur antecedentium gregem, pergentes, non *qua* eundum est, sed qua *itur*.

SENECA *de vita beata* ; Cap. I.

I. *Gedanken von der wahren Schätzung der lebendigen Kräfte.*—Reflections upon the true computation of living (moving) powers. Königsberg, 220 pp. large 8vo. with two plates, 1746.

After having paid handsome and due compliments to his meritorious countrymen LEIBNITZ, WOLF, HERRMANN, BERNOULLI, BULLFINGER, and many other eminent philosophers, the young author examines the different theories and proofs advanced " on the living (inherent) powers of bodies," and endeavours to shew, that *their* notions on this intricate subject were far from being correct, and that the dissentions prevailing among them arose chiefly from having, each of them, considered the subject in a different point of view. Thus their understandings were misled by paying an undue regard, partly to the *obstacles overcome by weight*; partly to *matter as acted upon, or moved, by weight*; partly to the *pressure suffered by elastic bodies*; and finally to the *velocities arising from compound motion*.—He attacks LEIBNITZ most severely, while he enters upon a fundamental inquiry into the origin of his theory concerning the moving powers. It appears obvious to KANT, that LEIBNITZ had been led to this theory, by implicitly proceeding on the known rule from which DESCARTES explains the nature of the lever. Prior to LEIBNITZ, the world had admitted the simple proposition of DESCARTES, " that the mere velocity of bodies, even such as are in actual motion, serves as a rule for ascertaining their power." But LEIBNITZ suddenly roused the reasoning powers of man, by proposing a new law which, since that period, has offered rich materials for discussion to the most learned and acute. DESCARTES had computed the powers of bodies in motion by *mere* velocity. But LEIBNITZ adopted the *square of velocities* in this computation.

Whatever

Whatever merit may be due, from this CHRONOLOGICAL ANALYSIS, *to the Recorder of* KANT'S COLLECTIVE WORKS, *and from having engaged in a task—perhaps the most toilsome in life;—I have still to lament the impossibility, or rather the impracticability of giving the respective contents of each work at full length; especially when I consider, both the limited size of these* ELEMENTS, *and the almost boundless region of* KANT'S *speculations.*

Nothing, therefore, but the well-founded hope, that no reasonable man will expect to find in these CONTENTS *more, or less, than I have promised,—can support me in this laborious undertaking.—*

CONTENTS.

CHAPTER FIRST. *Of the power of bodies, in general.* § 1. Every mechanical body possesses an *essential* power. 2. This power of bodies LEIBNITZ expressed by the common name, *effective power.* 3. It ought to be called *vis motrix* (moving power). 4. On the method of explaining motion from the effective powers in general. 5. Of the difficulties arising from the theory of reciprocal operation of body and mind, if we attribute to the former no other power, than the *vis motrix.* 6. Of the obstacles thence arising in the explanation of the manner, in which the mind affects the body; of the method of removing them, if we adopt a common *vis activa.* 7. There may exist things, the presence of which cannot be at all demonstrated. 8. It is not improbable, in a strict metaphysical sense, that there may be more than *one* world. 9. If bodies, or substances, had no power to operate *externally*, there would be neither *extension* nor *space.* 10. The *triple* dimension of space is probably derived from the law, according to which the powers of substances affect each other 11. Of the condition which renders the existence of a plurality of worlds probable. 12. Some Metaphysicians maintain, that bodies, by means of their (peculiar) powers, incline towards motion in all directions 13, 14. Two objections against this opinion: a.) That the moving body does not advance in an equal ratio with the body moved; b.) That the effort towards motion, which substances manifest in all directions, must have a certain degree of intensity; for it cannot be infinite, and a finite (limited) exertion, without a certain degree of effort, involves a contradiction. 15. Motion must be considered to be of *two* different kinds. 16 Motion of the *first* kind is analogous to dead (inert) pressure. 17. 18. 19. Motion of the second kind presupposes a power, which corresponds with the square of velocity

CHAPTER SECOND. *Inquiry into the principles, upon which the adherents of* LEIBNITZ *explain the living powers.* § 20, 21 BUELFINGER's advice in settling differences between parties 22 LEIBNITZ's and DESCARTES's method of computing powers. 23. *First* error of LEIBNITZ, in asserting " if a body is in actual motion his power is equal to the square of its velocity." 24. Actual motion is that, which is not merely at the point of beginning, but during which a certain time has elapsed. This intermediate time, between the beginning of motion and the moment in which the body moves, properly conflitutes what is called *actual motion*. 25. *Second* error of Leibnitz, " that the time consumed during motion is the true and only character of living power, and that from this alone the difference of computing dead and living powers must result." 26. Further proof against Leibnitz, from the law of continuity. 27. The time elapsed during motion, consequently the reality of motion, is not the true criterion of computing the living power of bodies. 28, 29. Mathematics cannot prove the reality of living powers. 30. Leibnitz was first misled in the computation of living powers, by Descartes's explanation of the lever. 31. HERRMANN's affertion, that the powers are in proportion to the heights, to which they may rife. 32. Refutation of this affertion. 33. The followers of Descartes commit the same error. 34, 35. LICHTSCHEID's doubts upon this head removed. 36. 37. 38. An instance which proves, that in the computation of power arising from weight, time must be necessarily taken into account. 39. Summary of all the proofs derived from the motion of elastic bodies. 40. The Leibnitzians refute their own conjectures, through the Systems of Mechanics which they establish. 41. Herrmann's statement, respecting the repulsion of three elastic bodies, examined. 42, 43. The origin of the fallacy in the reasoning, by which he established his conclusion. 44. This conclusion was unknown to *Mad. de* CHASTELET. 45, 46, 47. JURIN's objection concerning the reciprocal pulsion of two elastic and unequal bodies;—BERNOUILLI's answer to this objection, in comparing it with the pressure suffered by elastic bodies;—his ideas on the subject are refuted by his *own* premises, which confirm KANT's opinion. 48. Defence of the living powers, supported by the constant balance of power in the world. 49, 50. Two different ways of explaining this affertion. 51. The source of Leibnitz's hypothesis relative to the preservation of a uniform power, with proposals for settling this controversy, and a conclusive answer to *his* affertion. 52. According to the law established by LEIBNITZ, the power exercised in the touch, between a small and a larger elastic body, is the same before as after this contact. 53. The fallacy of this observation itself refutes the theory of the living powers, as maintained by the Leibnitzians. 54. This appears still more obvious, by inverting the case; if, namely, a larger elastic body is brought into contact with a smaller one. 55. Calculation affords proofs of the Cartesian law, that " if a larger body touches a smaller one, there remains an equal proportion of power." 56. The power, with which a smaller body recoils from a larger one, is called *minus*. 57. Mad. de CHASTELET has very improperly ridiculed this determination, which *M. de* MAIRAN first proposed. 58. The Leibnitzians shrink from the inquiry into the living powers, by means of the pulsion observed in *unelastic* bodies. 59. The latter is more decisive in determining the living powers, than the resistance of elastic bodies. 60, 61. The Leibnitzians give a frivolous answer to these objections, by saying, that " in the repulsion of unelastic bodies, one half of the power is consumed in the impression

made

made upon the parts of these bodies." 62. Reply *first*: because this is a mechanical, not a mathematical effect of bodies. 63. Reply *second*: because we have no right to call a body unelastic, tho' it be perfectly hard. 64. Reply *third*: the impression made upon the parts, offers no argument for asserting, that a part of the power of unelastic bodies is lost by the resistance exerted on their side. 65. Reply *fourth*: the degree of hardness in unelastic bodies, and the degree of power exerted in the contact, must yet be determined by the Leibnitzians. 66. The resistance of unelastic bodies entirely destroys the living powers. 67—70. General proof, that the concussion of elastic bodies must, in every instance, evince the falsity of supposing living powers;—that in the percussion of elastic bodies we ought to consider only the *incipient* velocity of the body *percussed*. 71==77. Examination of the proofs of the living powers derived from compound motion: particularly BUELFINGER's, which is refuted in several ways. 78. The straight power in the diagonal line does not correspond with the amount of power exerted towards the lateral parts. 79. In the computation of power by LEIBNITZ, the amount of it, in an oblique direction, is equal to the diagonal power; but in that by DESCARTES, the former frequently is infinitely greater than the latter. 80==83. A new case towards the refutation of living powers; viz. " that a body moving in a circle produces the same effect, with respect to gravity, as if it reclined upon an oblique surface;—and that a circular moving body, in every finite measure of *time*, produces the effect of a finite *power*, even against the obstacles of *gravity*. 84. DESCARTES removes this difficulty by his method of computing power. 85. Another contradiction in this computation by the square; for every one agrees " that the computed power of velocity resulting from the multiplication with itself, according to the right angle, must have infinitely more force, than that which is simply expressed by the measure of velocity; and that it has the some relation to this, as the surface has to the line." 86. The case stated by BERNOUILLI, concerning the *elastic* power of *four similar* springs, is here refuted. 87==90. MAIRAN's objection against the statement of HERRMANN; the utility of the method adopted by the former; its tendency to prevent certain palpable mistakes, which have long remained concealed. 91. BUELFINGER's distinctions, by which he endeavours to elude the objection of MAIRAN, are settled by this method. 92, 93. A singular compound case by LEIBNITZ, which rests upon fallacious reasoning.

" As BERNOUILLI, HERRMANN and WOLF, the admirers of LEIBNITZ, have
" not, in the usual manner, informed us—that *nothing* equals this proof in point of
" invention and (apparent) strength.—I am inclined to think, ' says Kant,' that
" so great a man as LEIBNITZ could not err, without gaining reputation by the
" very idea, that misled him into this error." I cannot, upon this occasion, forget
" the words of HECTOR in VIRGIL :

―――― ―――― Si Pergama dextra
Defendi possent, etiam hae defensa fuissent.

Virg. Aeneid.

94, 95. The power, which the body A has acquired by the arrangement of a
machine

machine, is *not* the effect of power produced by the body B. 96. The same is confirmed from the law of *continuity*. 97. The whole extent of the *sufficient reason* in the preceding position. 98. The only difficulty, that still prevails in the Leibnitzian argument, is answered. 99. PAPIN's evasive objection is weak and untenable, viz. "*Quomodo autem per translationem totius potentiæ corporis A in corpus B, juxta Cartesium, obtineri possit motus perpetuus evidentissime demonstrat, atque ita Cartesianos ad absurdum reductos arbitratur. Ego autem et motum perpetuum absurdum esse fateor, et Cl. Vir. demonstrationem ex supposita translatione esse legitimam.*" And after having, in this *positive manner*, declared himself against that important position of DESCARTES, he seeks for shelter, in disputing the premises of his adversary; and in challenging *him*, to solve this *Gordian knot*. The following words discover his opinion: *Sed Hypothesis ipsius possibilitatem translationis nimirum totius potentiæ ex corpore A in corpus B pernego, etc. (Act. Erudit. 1691. page 9.)*—100—101. LEIBNITZ's reply to PAPIN is equally inconsistent, and KANT believes that the former has written these words in good earnest: "*Cum Florentiæ essem, dedi amico aliam adhuc demonstrationem, pro possibilitate translationis virium dotalium, &c. corpore majore in minus quiescens, prorsus affinem iis ipsis, quo Cl. Papinus ingenuosissime pro me juvando excogitavit, pro quibus gratias debeo, imo et ago, sinceritate ejus dignas.*"—Proof, that a quadruple body may communicate to a single body four degrees of velocity by means of percussion upon a lever;—how PAPIN ought to have reasoned against LEIBNITZ; all the arguments for proving the entity of living powers against the computation of Descartes have failed; no hopes are left to to reconcile them. 102. The principal arguments of the Leibnitzians refuted. 103, 104. WOLF's argument, and his principal axiom: " if a body has passed through the same space, it has also produced the same *innocuous effect*." 105. Another axiom of the *Wolfian Schediasma*: " As spaces (objects of space), in the act of uniform motion, bear a compound relation to the velocities and times; so the *innocuous effects* correspond with the masses, times, and velocities of bodies." Upon this axiom, WOLF establishes the following erroneous theorem: *Actiones quibus idem effectus producitur, sunt et celeritates*. 106. We are not yet in the possession of a *System of Dynamicks*. 107, 108. The argument of MUSCHENBROEK examined. 109. A new case for the confirmation of the Cartesian method of computing powers. 110. The doubts of Leibnitz solved by Jurin. 111, 112. Mad. de Chastelet's frivolous objection against Jurin's argument exposed. 113. RICHTER's objections share the same fate.—The author concludes this Chapter with some supplementary notes and illustrations, in which he unfolds the following particulars: (a) Why the undetermined idea of finite time, also includes the portion of time infinitely small? (b) Leibnitz's method of computing powers cannot even be admitted under the condition of finite (limited) velocity. (c) Why time must necessarily enter into the computation of the obstacles occasioned by gravity.

CHAPTER THIRD. *A view of a new method of computing the living powers; being the only true measure of natural powers.*—§. 114. That law, which has been found inapplicable in *Mathematics*, may nevertheless apply to Natural Philosophy. 115. Distinction between *mathematical* and *natural* bodies, and between the laws relative to both. 116. Velocity affords no just idea of power. 117. There would be no power, if there were no effort to preserve the *status in se*; illustration of the idea of *intension*. 118. If intension be comparable with a *point*, power resembles a line, namely that of velocity. 119. If intension be finite, i. e. like a line, *power* is comparable with a *square*. 120. A body, that manifests an internal effort to preserve its motion free and constant, has a power analagous to the square of velocity. 121. A body cannot acquire its living power from without. 122. There is an infinite number of intermediate degrees between dead and living power;—the latter can arise only in a finite time, after the beginning of motion. 123. That state, in which the power of bodies is not yet *living* (evolved), but is in a progressive crisis, KANT terms the *vivification*. 124, 125. According to a new estimation of powers, a body that preserves its velocity, in free motion, *in infinitum* undiminished, possesses living power, i. e. such a power as can be estimated by the square of velocity. 126. As there are free motions, there are likewise living powers.—Mathematics admit no free motions. 127. An easier method of applying these reflections to advantage. 128. BERNOUILLI was not unacquainted with these ideas, " *Vis viva*," says he, " *est aliquid reale et substantiale, quod per se subsistit, et quantum in se est, non dependit ab alio:* ——————— *Vis mortua non est aliquid absolutum et per se durans*, &c. 129. The living powers are of an accidental nature. 130, 131. Experience confirms the successive *vivification*. 132, 133. Vivification is not applicable to all velocities in general;—application of this rule to motion, in a resisting medium. 134, 135. Whether vivification and free motion, in all the higher degrees of velocity, are possible *in infinitum*. 136—138. The living power may in part vanish, without having produced any effect. 139, 140. The phenomena of those bodies which overcome gravity, neither manifest any living power, nor do they militate against it. 141. Soft bodies do not operate with their collective power. 142, 143. Query: whether the effect of bodies, without distinction, is proportional to the mass of their living power. 144, 145. The mass, in which a body can produce effects proportional to its living power, must be determined; smaller masses, under a certain size, cannot produce that effect. 146, 147. Fluid bodies operate in proportion to the square of velocity. 148—151. The motions of elastic bodies are inconsistent with the computation of Leibnitz, but they agree with that of Kant. 152, 153. Mechanical proof of the living powers, by MUSCHENBROEK. 154, 155. A spring of equal elasticity communicates a greater degree of power to a larger body than to a smaller one. 156—158. Whence the squares of velocities of cylinders are in an inverse ratio to the masses. 159—161. In the effect of gravity, time ought to be computed;—soft substances are of a very different nature. 162. The force of resistance of soft matter takes place with finite velocity.

II. *Allgemeine Naturgeschichte, oder Theorie des Himmels, nach Newtonischen Grundsätzen.* A general history of nature, or theory of the heavens, upon Newtonian principles. 8vo. *Koenigsberg.* 1755.

III.

III. *Principiorum metaphysicorum nova dilucidatio.* 4to. 1755.

IV. *Dissertatio de principiis primis cognitionis humanæ.* 4to. *Regiomonti* 1755.

V. *Monadologia physica.* 4to. 1756.

VI. *Geschichte der merkwürdigsten Vorfälle des Erdbebens, welches am Ende des 1755 sten Jahres einen grossen Theil der Erde erschüttert hat.*—History of the most remarkable events produced by the earthquake, which convulsed a great part of the globe, towards the end of the year 1755. 4to. *Koenigsberg,* 1756.

VII. *Neuer Lehrbegriff der Bewegung und Ruhe, und der damit verknüpften Erfahrungen in der Naturwissenschaft.*—New theory of motion and rest, together with an account of the experiments relative to them in Natural Philosophy. 4to. *Koenigsberg.* 1758.

VIII. *Betrachtungen über den Optimismus.*—Reflections upon Optimism. 4to. 1759.

IX. *Entwurf und Ankündigung eines Collegii der physischen Geographie, nebst einer Untersuchung: ob die Westwinde in unsern Gegenden darum feucht sind, weil sie über ein grosses Meer streichen?*—A sketch and annunciation of a course of lectures on physical geography; together with an inquiry whether the westerly winds are for this reason moist in our climate, because they blow over a great sea. 4to. *Koenigsberg.* 1759.

X. *Erweis der falschen Spitzfindigkeit der vier syllogistischen Figuren.*—The false subtleties of the four syllogistical figures proved. 8vo. 1762.

XI. *Versuch, den Begriff der negativen Grössen in die Weltweisheit einzuführen.*—An attempt towards introducing the idea of negative magnitudes into philosophy. 1763.

XII. *Einzig möglicher Beweisgrund zu einer Demonstration*

des

des Daseyns Gottes. The only possible method of proving the existence of the Deity. 8vo. *Koenigsberg.* 1763.

XIII. *Beobachtungen über das Gefübl des Schönen und Erhabenen.* Observations upon the effect of the Beautiful and Sublime. 8vo. *Koenigsberg.* 1764. 2d Edit. 1770.

XIV. *Träume eines Geistersehers, erläutert durch Träume der Metaphysik.* Dreams of a Fanatic, illustrated by dreams in Metaphysics. 8vo. 1764.

XV. *Abhandlung über die Evidenz in Metaphysischen Wissenschaften; die bey der Königlichen Akademie der Wissenschaften das Accessit erhalten hat, und mit Moses Mendelsohns Preisschrift zugleich erschienen ist.* A Treatise on Evidence in Metaphysical Sciences, &c. 8vo. *Berlin.* 1764.

XVI. *Anmerkungen zur Erläuterung der Theorie der Winde.* Remarks serving to illustrate the theory of the winds. 4to. 1765.

Of these works, the reader will scarcely require a detailed account; for the most of them, though several times reprinted, have become very scarce. They are indeed, in some degree, connected with the following systematic works of the author; but as Professor Kant has not strictly adopted that method of demonstration, which he *first* proposed in the publication stated under No. XII. viz. " The only possible method of proving the existence of the Deity," I considered it as an unprofitable task to translate the Indexes belonging to these respective works; though it were in my power to procure them from Germany. For the same reason, I presume, Mr. NITSCH has remarked in his late excellent publication, " A general and introductory view of Prof. Kant's principles concerning man, the world, and the Deity;" that the work above alluded to, No. XII, does not constitute any part of the Kantean System, as the first edition of it was published ten years(or from the first Edition of it, eighteen years) before that system was completed.

XVII. (1) *De Mundi sensibilis atque intelligibilis forma et principiis.* Dissertatio pro loco professionis Log. et Metaph.

taph. ordinariæ rite sibi vindicando; quam exigentibus statutis academicis publice tuebitur IMMANUEL KANT.— *Regiomonti*, in auditori maximo, horis matutinis et pomeridianis confuetis; Die XX. Aug. MDCCLXX.

SECTIO I. *De notione mundi generatim.*—Momenta, in mundi definitione attendenda, hæc funt: 1 *Materia* (in senfu tranfcendentali) h. e. *partes*, quæ hic fumuntur effe *fubftantiæ*. 2. *Forma* quæ confiftit in fubftantiarum *coordinatione*, non fubordinatione. 3. *Univerfitas* quæ eft omnitudo compartium *abfoluta*.

SECTIO II. *De fenfibilium atque intelligibilium difcrimine generatim.*—*Senfualitas* eft *receptivitas* fubjecti, per quam poffibile eft, ut ftatus ipfius repræfentativus objecti alicujus præfentia certo modo afficiatur. Intelligentia (rationalitas) eft *facultas* fubjecti, per quam, quæ in fenfus ipfius per qualitatem fuam, incurrere non poffunt, fibi repræfentare valet.

SECTIO III. *De principiis formæ Mundi fenfibilis.*—De TEMPORE. 1. *Idea Temporis* non oritur fed *fupponitur* a fenfibus. 2. Idea Temporis eft *fingularis*, non generalis: Tempus enim quodlibet non cogitatur, nifi tanquam pars unius ejufdem temporis immenfi. 3. Idea itaque temporis eft *intuitus*, et quoniam ante omnem fenfationem concipitur, tanquam conditio refpectuum in fenfibilibus obviorum, eft *intuitus*, non fenfualis, fed *purus*. 4. Tempus eft *quantum continuum* et legum continui in mutationibus univerfi principium. 5. *Tempus non eft objectivum aliquid et reale*, nec fubftantia, nec accidens, nec relatio, fed fubjectiva conditio per naturam mentis humanæ neceffaria, quælibet fenfibilia, certa lege fibi coordinandi, et *intuitus purus*. 6. Tempus eft conceptus veriffimus, et, per omnia poffibilia fenfuum objecta, in infinitum patens, intuitivæ repræfentationis conditio. 7. Tempus itaque eft *principium formale Mundi fenfibilis* abfolute primum.—De SPATIO. A. Conceptus fpatii non abftrahitur a fenfationibus externis. B. Conceptus fpatii eft fingularis reprefentatio omnia *in fe* comprehendens, non *fub fe* continens notio abftracta et communis. C. Conceptus fpatii itaque eft *intuitus purus*; cum fit conceptus fingularis, fenfationibus non conflatus, fed omnis fenfationis externæ forma fundamentalis. D. *Spatium non eft aliquid objectivi* et realis, nec fubftantia, nec accidens, nec relatio; fed fubjectivum et ideale et a natura

tura

tura mentis ſtabili lege proficiſcens, veluti ſchema, omnia omnino externe ſenſa ſibi coordinandi. E. Quanquam *conceptus ſpatii*, ut objectivi alicujus et realis entis vel affectionis, ſit imaginarius, nihilo tamen ſecius, *reſpective ad ſenſibilia quæcunque*, non ſolum eſt *veriſſimus*, ſed et omnis veritatis in ſenſualitate externa fundamentum.

SECTIO IV. *De principio formæ mundi intelligibilis.*

SECTIO V. *De methodo circa ſenſitiva et intellectualia in Metaphyſicis.*

Concerning the laſt two Sections, I cannot omit mentioning, that an abſtract of them could not be rendered intelligible to the reader, without ſtating likewiſe the illuſtrations of the different poſitions, at full length. Of this detail, the preſent ſketch will not admit; eſpecially as the principles, reſulting from the diſquiſitions contained in theſe two Sections, have been already expounded in the *five problems*, which conſtitute the principal part of the preſent *Elements*; and which, I have reaſon to hope, will afford a comprehenſive, though ſuccinct, view of KANT's CRITIQUE.—No further apology will be required by the learned, that the preceding extract from the author's *Inaugural Diſſertation* has been given in his own words, in the original Latin; for, to tranſlate this into Engliſh, might be conſidered as an inſult offered to the literati of this country.—With reſpect to the ſubſequent works, it muſt be remembered, that our object is merely to exhibit the contents of thoſe, which could be procured from Germany, during the limited intercourſe with that country, and to define the moſt difficult and abſtruſe terms in the *Gloſſary*, which concludes this publication.

XVIII. (2) *Kritik der reinen Vernunft.* Critique of Pure Reaſon. 8vo. *Riga.* 1781. Second Edition improved, 1787. Third Edition 1790. Fourth Edition, 1794. pp. 884, and xliv pages Preface.

Table of Contents.

INTRODUCTION. I. Of the diſtinction between pure and empirical knowledge. II. We are in the poſſeſſion of certain <u>intuitions</u> (truths) *a priori*, and even common ſenſe never is without them. III. Philoſophy demands a ſcience, which may determine the poſſibility, the principles, and the extent of our intuitions *a priori*.

IV.

IV. Of the distinction between analytical and synthetical judgments. V. In all the theoretical sciences of reasoning we meet with synthetical judgments *a priori*, which are contained in them as principles. VI. General problem of Pure Reason. VII. Plan and division of a particular science, under the name of a Critique of Pure reason.

I. TRANSCENDENTAL ELEMENTARY DOCTRINE. *Part* I. Transcendental Aesthetic. *Sect.* I. Of space. II. Of time.—*Part* II. Transcendental Logic. *Introd.* Definition of transcendental Logic. 1. Of Logic in general. 2. Of transcendental Logic. 3. Of the division of general Logic, into Analysis and Dialectic. 4. Of the division of transcendental Logic, into transcendental Analysis and Dialectic.

DIVISION I. *Transcendental Analysis.*—BOOK I. Analysis of notions. *Chap.* I. Of the method of discovering all purely intellectual notions. *Sect.* I. Of the use of Logic in general. II. Of the logical function of the intellect, in judgments. III. Of the purely intellectual notions or Categories. *Chap.* II. Of the deduction of the purely intellectual notions. *Sect.* I. Of the principles of a transcendental deduction in general. II. Transcendental deduction of the purely intellectual notions. BOOK II. Analysis of principles (transcendental doctrine of the judging faculty).—*Introd.* Of the transcendental judging faculty in general. *Chap.* I. Of the schema of the pure notions of the intellect. II. System of all the principles of the pure intellect. *Sect.* I. Of the supreme principle of all analytical judgments. II. Of the supreme principle of all synthetical judgments. III. Systematic exhibition of all synthetical principles of the pure intellect. 1. Axioms of perception. 2. Anticipations of apperception (observation). 3. Analogies of experience. a.) The principle of continuity of substance. b.) The principle of succession in time. c.) The principle of coexistence.—4. Postulates of empirical thought in general. *Chap.* I. Of the ground of distinction between all objects in general, into phenomena and *noumena*.—Of the ambiguity arising in the ideas of reflection, by confounding the empirical use of the intellect with that of the transcendental.

DIVISION II. *Transcendental Dialectic.* *Introd.* I. Of transcendental illusion. II. Of Pure Reason being the seat of transcendental illusion. a.) Of Reason in general. b.) Of the logical use of reason. c.) Of the pure use of reason. Book I. Of the notions afforded by Pure Reason. *Sect*. I. Of ideas in general. II. Of transcendental ideas. III. System of transcendental ideas. Book II. Of the dialectic conclusions of Pure Reason. *Chap*. I. Of the false conclusions of Pure Reason, respecting their form (*paralogismi*). Of the antinomy of Pure Reason. *Sect*. I. System of the cosmological ideas. II. Antithesis of Pure Reason. III. Of the interest of reason in this contest with itself. IV. Of the transcendental problems of Pure Reason, in so far as they must necessarily be solved. V. Sceptical exhibition of the cosmological questions, through all four transcendental ideas. VI. Transcendental Idealism, being the key to the solution of cosmological Dialectic. VII. Critical decision of the cosmological contest, into which reason falls with itself. VIII. Regulative principle of Pure Reason, with respect to the cosmological ideas. IX. Of the empirical use of the regulative principle of reason, with respect to all cosmological ideas.—1. Solution of the cosmological idea respecting the totality of the composition of the phenomena of a whole universe. 2. Solution of the cosmological idea respecting the totality of division of a given whole in perception.—Concluding remark on the solution of the transcendental ideas in Mathematics; and previous remark on the solution of the transcendental ideas in Dynamics. 3. Solution of the cosmological idea respecting the totality of deriving the events of the world from their causes.—On the possibility of causality by the idea of liberty, as combined with the general law of physical necessity.—Illustration of the cosmological idea of a liberty, that is connected with the general laws of physical necessity. 4. Solution of the cosmological idea respecting the totality of the dependence of the phenomena, according to the reality of their existence in general. *Chap*. III. The *Prototype* of Pure Reason, i. e. an idea of reason *in concreto*. *Sect*. I. Of the prototype in general. II. Of the transcendental prototype. III. Of the arguments of speculative reason, to conclude the existence of a highest Being. IV. Of the impossibility of an ontological proof of the existence of God. V. Of the impossibility of a cosmological

mological proof of the existence of God. VI. Of the impossibility of a physico-theological proof. VII. Critique of all Theology from speculative principles of reason.—Of the final purpose of the natural Dialectic of human reason.

II. TRANSCENDENTAL DOCTRINE OF METHOD. *Chap.* I. The Discipline of Pure Reason. *Sect.* I. With respect to its dogmatical use. II. With respect to its polemical use. III. With respect to its hypotheses. IV. With respect to its proofs. *Chap.* II. The Canon of Pure Reason. *Sect.* I. Of the ultimate purpose of the pure use of Reason. II. Of the prototype of the highest good, as being the fundamental cause of determining the ultimate purpose of pure reason. III. On the expressions, " to be of opinion; to know; and to believe." *Chap.* III. Of the Architectonic of Pure Reason. *Chap.* IV. The history of Pure Reason.

Although we have already given the substance of this work in the *Problems*, which are exhibited in the foregoing part of these Elements; yet in a matter of such importance as the present attempt of KANT actually is, we do not hesitate to insert here another exposition of his principles, so that the reader may acquire a complete analytical view of their origin.

In order to trace the principles of all human knowledge and judgment, from what source both may arise, Kant deemed it incumbent upon the enquirer, to institute an accurate analysis of the intuitive faculty of man. The chief object of this inquiry was, 1, to separate the notion we have of the *intuitive faculty*, from all other notions connected with it; 2, to lay aside, or to abstract from, the concomitant and accidental characters of it; and to retain in this notion merely those characters, without which no intuitive faculty can at all be conceived: thus he obtained a general notion of the intuitive faculty of man, i. e. such as consists of no foreign ingredients. This faculty is the attribute of every man, it is given him in his own personal consciousness, and the reality of it cannot be proved otherwise than by an appeal to this consciousness. The existence of such a faculty has never been called in question, it is granted by all parties, and hence it is to be considered as a fair point, from which the philosopher may begin his inquiries.— To premise a definition of the intuitive faculty, is by no means necessary; for its reality will be sufficiently proved, if the constituent parts and characters produced of it, be of such a nature as can be discovered in every individual, who has the requisite capacity and inclination of reflecting upon the successive operations of his mind. Of infinitely greater importance we shall find the complete analysis of this faculty; since the definition of something, the truth of which cannot be discovered otherwise than by the preceding operation, can be of no positive advantage.

KANT seriously discovered, that the intuitive faculty of man is a compound of very dissimilar ingredients; or, in other words, that it consists of parts very different in their nature, and each of which performs functions peculiar to itself; namely the *Sensitive Faculty*, and the *Understanding*. The former represents the matter of things, so as it is affected by them; the latter connects the variety of these materials into a whole. These two operations must always precede, if there shall take place a representation or intuition of a determined object. Both, therefore, are essential constituents of the intuitive faculty of man, and both must be active, at the same time, in every intuition.

LEIBNITZ, indeed, had likewise remarked the distinction subsisting between the Sensitive Faculty and the Understanding; but he entirely overlooked the essential difference between their functions, and was of opinion, that both faculties were different from one another only in degree, while he supposed the Sensitive Faculty to be only a weaker degree of the Intuitive, which, when operating in a stronger degree, was called the Understanding: both, according to him, represented the same objects, save that the Sensitive Faculty exhibited those objects in a confused and obscure manner, which the Understanding precisely and clearly apprehended. But this distinction is altogether false and without foundation. The Understanding, as far as we can explore this faculty, still remains, even in its weakest degree, essentially different from the Sensitive Faculty, and the most perfect functions of the latter can never supply the functions of the Understanding. For, while the senses receive the matter of the objects, the Understanding combines the variety in that matter, and forms a determined representation of an object, or an intuition. The former may receive clear or obscure impressions; the latter may also combine in a distinct or confused manner. Clearness and obscurity, distinctness and confusion, may, therefore, be common to both; nay, what is clearly perceived by the senses, may yet be obscurely apprehended by the Understanding; and what the former exhibit in a confused and obscure manner, may nevertheless be very clearly conceived by the latter. The Understanding may even form a clear notion of things, that never can become objects of sense; and *vice versa*, the senses may perceive things, which the understanding cannot represent, either clearly or obscurely; although it is impossible to have an intuition of any one object, unless both faculties are actively concerned in the same object. For instance, to *think* of God, liberty, virtue, and immortality, cannot yet be called to *recognise* or to have an intuition of the objects, different from their ideas; and to perceive spaces and times, and sensible objects of all kinds, can likewise not be said to have intuitions of them. For, to acquire the latter, we must reduce the objects to ideas, and combine them according to certain laws. The senses can do nothing further than perceive, i. e. represent the given thing *immediately*; and the understanding only can think of it, i. e. combine the thing perceived, or exhibit the given thing by *mediately* connecting it into one. The reality of the object, that is conceived by us in an idea, can be represented only by the senses, since the object itself is either perceived through the sensation occasioned by it, or it must necessarily be combined with any one perception, according to the laws of possible experience.

In the works of the English and French philosophers, we find this essential distinction between the sensitive and the intellectual faculties, and their combination towards producing one synthetical intuition, scarcely mentioned. LOCKE only alludes to the accidental limitations of both faculties; but to inquire into the essential difference prevailing between them, does not at all occur to him. It is, however, obvious, that from this neglect there have arisen many fallacious conclusions, which for a long time, at least in their consequences, have been hurtful to sound philosophy.

This distinction then, between the sensitive and intellectual faculties, forms an essential feature in the philosophy of Kant; it is

the

the basis, upon which the most of the subsequent inquiries are established. It must nevertheless be remembered, that Kant, in distinguishing these two faculties, does not speak of real substances, different from one another. His intention merely is, to point out what every reflecting mind may easily observe within himself, if he attends to what precedes an intuition, and how the understanding combines every act of perception. Now, since the ground or source of these two faculties obviously discovers two distinct powers, it is both rational and necessary, to denote their functions by distinct names; though their essentially different operations should be formed in one and the same substance. We cannot attend here to an inference, that may be drawn from this identity of origin, against the discrimination of powers, that are in themselves as distinct as the motion of a clock is from that of the hammer, which strikes the bell, though by the same mechanism, that moves the pendulum and the hands. In this very contrivance, we may find the most convincing instance of the actual difference between the exercise of the sensitive and intellectual faculties, if we consider it both, in an *objective* and *subjective* view. In the former, we behold no more than a machine that moves, at certain equal distances, the hands which are attached to it; and he, who is unacquainted with the purpose for which it is designed, will view it with the astonishment and fear of the Swiss peasant, who formerly destroyed a time-piece dropped by a traveller, because he apprehended mischief from the noise that accompanied its motion. But, if this untutored son of nature had been informed of the great utility of that machine, by the construction of which mankind have contrived to measure time apparent, his intellectual faculty might thus have been enlarged, and he would have acquired the *subjective* view of a watch. Without having had any previous experience of the design, with which the motions of a time-piece are arranged *in spaces*, he could now conceive, *a priori*, the necessary result of this arrangement, by dividing the duration of the day into hours, minutes, and seconds; although experience would *a posteriori* confirm this intuitive notion, and give it *objective reality*. This, indeed, cannot be obtained in any other way than by means of the senses; for the question, here, is not of the last and absolute ground or substance of the intuitive faculty, but concerning the intuitive faculty as an appeal to this last substratum, that is determined by its operations.—Thus Copernicus acquired demonstrative certainty upon what he, at first, had conceived only as an hypothesis; for the central laws of the motions of celestial bodies at the same time proved the reality of that invisible power of attraction, which supports the fabric of the universe, and which Newton never could have discovered, if the former had not ventured to go beyond the limits of possible experience, and to search for the ground or cause of the motions observed, not in the objects of the celestial bodies, but in the eyes of the spectator.

Kant, therefore, previously analysed the Sensitive Faculty, and endeavoured to discover the necessary conditions, without which our Sensitive Faculty cannot perceive any objects whatever. After having cautiously separated all that, which, in the phenomena exhibited by the senses, either is merely accidental, or is owing to the function of the intellect, he discovered, that *two conditions* only remain, without which, every where, neither our Sensitive Faculty, nor its objects, are conceivable. These conditions are, *Space* and *Time*. They have ever been the stumbling block of all metaphysicians, and the source of endless disputes. Kant considers them in such a manner as will afford satisfaction to every cool and unbiassed enquirer after truth, since none but the most inveterate Sceptic, or the obstinate Systematic, can withhold their assent. He shows namely,

1, That both these representations are the immediate productions of the senses, and consequently admit of no further derivation. Hence it was a fruitless attempt of Leibnitz, who endeavoured to explain their origin from intellectual notions. The Understanding has, indeed, the power of arranging Space and Time with their modifications, under the ideas of order, unity, and so forth, but it cannot derive either of them from these ideas; it can unfold and explain their contents, but it cannot conceive the possibility of their origin, any further than that they are something given us by the Sensitive Faculty itself.

2, They must be thought of as the substratum of all sensible objects, i. e. as the forms of all phenomena. But they are not real objects and self-subsistent, as Clarke imagined: their reality

wholly

wholly depends upon those things, which can be observed in them, abstractly considered, they are the bare forms of our Sensitive Faculty; forms, through which we are enabled to determine, that all real objects of sense are conformable to them, or that these objects must of necessity be given in them.—It is by this manner of representation, that we can explain *all* the predicates of Space and Time, as that of infinity, continuity, uniformity, &c. without incurring those difficulties, which have been productive of the greatest confusion in philosophy, and which have involved Mathematics and Metaphysics into perpetual dissensions.

3, Finally, Kant also shows, that space and time, being the forms of *our* Sensitive Faculty, must consequently be conceived as the forms of those objects only, of which *we* can attain intuitions; thus they are merely forms of phenomena, and not the forms of all things in general, that are the objects of knowledge. Nay, it is even conceivable, that the things exhibited to us in space and time, abstractly considered, may be viewed or perceived by other thinking beings, under very different forms; although it is not in our power, either to determine more precisely this difference, or to ascertain the real possibility of it, by any arguments favourable to this conjecture.

From the preceding statement, the reader will be able to form a general idea of the manner, in which the universal truths of Mathematics may be demonstrated upon the principles of the Critical philosopher, and how these principles may be employed, to determine thereby the objects of the world of sense. For, since space and time are apprehended immediately through the nature of our sensitive faculty, it is now conceivable; how we can perceive all their relations, compare them with one another through the understanding, and deduce general principles from these sources. And as all the objects of sense necessarily appear in these forms, the explanation is self-evident, that all the relations apprehended *a priori*, must also necessarily be discovered in all these phenomena. It likewise follows from this illustration, that all Mathematics consist in a science, relating only to objects of sense, and admitting of no application whatever, to those of an opposite nature.

After having satisfactorily proved, that there are neither more nor fewer of the neceſſary conditions of perception in the Senſitive Faculty, than Space and Time, Kant proceeds to the inveſtigation of the Underſtanding, as the ſecond principal conſtituent of the intuitive Faculty. He remarks, that all the operations of the underſtanding may be ultimately reduced to the *act of judging*, and he concludes from this, that the different modifications in a judgment, in general, are the principles, according to which the pure notions of the intellect muſt be determined. Upon this ground, he previouſly unfolds all the ſimple and pure notions of the intellect, and exhibits them, in a complete and ſyſtematic manner, as the ultimate elements of all judgments.—It is well known, how much the ſimple notions or firſt principles have intereſted the Metaphyſicians of all ages; it is alſo known, that they never could agree with reſpect to their number; whether, among the ſimple or primary notions, there had not been included ſome of a compound nature; whether thoſe conſidered as original ones were not at the bottom merely derivatives; whether there is no chance of diſcovering in future a greater number of ſimple notions, or of reducing thoſe already diſcovered to a ſmaller number. All theſe doubts and diſputes, Kant has now terminated, by diſcovering a principle, from which it appears evident, that there can be neither more nor fewer than *twelve* * originally pure notions of the underſtanding.

The way, in which Kant diſcovers theſe Categories or primary notions, and how he proves their completeneſs and validity, cannot be detailed nor abridged in this general retroſpect of the Critique; but I ſhall briefly remark, that the categories exactly compriſe thoſe notions, without which the underſtanding is unable to conceive any objects whatever, i. e. to judge of them. Hence they expreſs nothing further than the mode or manner, how the Underſtanding, by the laws of its conſtitution, muſt neceſſarily combine the varities in perception, whenever it attempts to judge upon objects. But the forms of objects naturally lie in the underſtanding, and as ſuch they have always been inveſtigated and determined

---

* See the Categories, p. 45, and compare them with the definitions in the *Gloſſary*.

termined in Logic. Thus the Logicians have long ago taught us, from the nature of the Understanding, that every judgment must be determined by its extent and compass, as well as by its relation to synthetic unity and consciousness; or that it must have a certain quantity, quality, relation, and modality. But that, through this process alone, the conceivable objects are determined, that consequently the forms of judgment are carried over to the objects of thought, and can be predicated of them *a priori*, this necessary inference has been less attended to, by former philosophers. For, though they have not failed to make use of the notions thus arising, in order to determine the objects *a priori*, yet the peculiar source of these notions has hitherto remained undiscovered.

From this source, Kant derives all our notions *a priori*, and makes them the predicates of general principles, which throughout, become the laws relative to objects of experience *a priori*; for they do not contain actual experience itself, but the general conditions, that render experience possible, between the nature of man and things. These laws are systematically exhibited in the CRITIQUE, agreeably to one principle, so that the reader is convinced, that there are neither more nor fewer of the general, necessary, and elementary principles, than are unfolded through this inquiry. But these principles are likewise the axioms of a physical science, so far as nature consists of nothing else but the whole complex of experimental objects; and consequently, from this idea of nature, we not only conceive, very perfectly, the possibility of reducing Physics to a scientific system, but likewise this system itself is, in its pure or transcendental part, thus actually formed.

Having stated in the preceding outlines, how our Understanding must represent to itself given objects, or how an intuition of them becomes possible through it, I can now proceed to the particular analysis of the intellectual faculty in forming conclusions, which Kant denominates *theoretical reason*. This branch of the intellectual faculty, by virtue of its constitution, produces certain notions to which no objects whatever correspond *in* experience, although they are connected *with* it in succession, and are both influenced and determined by experience. It is namely, in general, the idea of the *unconditional* or *absolute*, that is immediately connected with

th

the nature of Reason, and through which, according to the different form of rational conclusions, the ideas of an absolute subject or *mind*, of an absolute cause or *liberty*, and of an absolute totality of all that is possible, i. e. the idea of *God*, take their respective origin. The further deduction of these notions, abstracted from pure Reason, must be studied from Kant's Critique; it forms one of the most excellent parts of that work. We learn from it, not only to understand completely, how all mankind, immediately after the evolution of their mental faculties, attain these ideas; but we likewise conceive, how the representations formed concerning the objects *i* these ideas, appear under so great a variety of aspects, as soon as we venture to determine the objects beyond the nature of the ideas founded upon human reason: nay, we can even generally understand, how variously these determinations may be modified. We further learn, that those, who endeavour to derive every thing concerning religion, from habit, education, and other accidental circumstances, judge with the partiality and fallacy of others, who consider their incidental opinions as incontrovertible principles, which are deduced from the essence of transcendental objects themselves, or to which they fondly would give the appearance of infallibility, by appealing to the authority of a divine inspiration. We also see, how easily the *accidental* may be confounded with the *necessary*, the *subjective* with the *objective*, the *natural* with the *artificial*; unless we are acquainted with the sources, from which all these objects flow, not only so far as their primary origin extends, but also with their minutest difference.— Without being enraged against those writers, who, from their assertions, appear to have formed the artful design of depriving man of every thing, that is valuable and interesting to him as a rational being, we can without difficulty conceive, that it is only a different interest or motive of our reason, which incites men to propagate irreligious doctrines; that it is not entirely their immoral will, but rather their too extensive views, encouraged by the weakness of their adversaries, that induce them to expose the arguments employed in favour of the most interesting principles of religion, while they flatter themselves with the prospect of controverting all the opinions of their opponents.

The CRITIQUE of KANT holds out the prospect of a most complete victory over all the enemies of Religion, and I shall now state, in what manner the principles of Religion are secured against all the attacks of its adversaries, and how religion is fortified against arbitrary and accidental additions. After having shown, that the ground of the idea concerning Mind, Liberty, and the Deity, is to be met with in the nature of Reason itself, and that every rational being is involuntarily led to the formation of these ideas, the author endeavours to prove, and he does this very satisfactorily, "*that the Intuitive Faculty of man has not the power of apprehending objects in a determined manner, or of pointing out characters of them, which are derived from immediate perception.*" He demonstrates, that we can indeed *think* the objects of these ideas, but that, at no time whatever, we are able to apprehend them *theoretically*. For, to acquire a theoretical idea of things, we must not only predicate of them, that they are conformable to the laws of our Understanding, or that they are not something contrary to them, but we must likewise be enabled to point out determinate and *real* predicates, which are taken from the thing itself under apprehension. But the real predicates of a thing cannot be conceived in any other manner, than through sensible perception; whether this take place by immediately perceiving the thing itself, or mediately through some other object, which has certain real properties, in common with that to be apprehended. Hence it follows, that we are unqualified to apprehend the real predicates, or the transcendental properties of those things, which, by their nature, neither in part nor in the whole, can ever become objects of sensible perception. We are altogether deficient in a faculty designed for that purpose; hence we are, for instance, unable to determine positively the nature of mind, according to its internal constitution. We can indeed predicate of it, with certainty, that it is not of itself an object of sense, consequently, not a phenomenon; but whatever predicates of reality may, in other respects, belong to it; how its existence may be constituted, whether it be a simple substance, and different from the internal absolute grounds of matter; how the idea of liberty is evolved; what properties belong to the Deity in a transcendental view, and the like; all these problems could be solved only through the perception of supersensible objects. And as we are provided with no faculty for the exercise of such a function, we cannot at all determine the real characters of these things; nay we do not even understand the real importance of the term "*existence*," when we apply it to superfensible objects. For, with respect to the objects of sense, the expression, "*something exists*," signifies no more than that it affects our senses, by producing a sensation, as soon as it is placed in proper connection with them. But the idea of existence cannot imply the same meaning with respect to superfensible objects; for the term "existence" is not to be defined in its bare relation to our Intuitive Faculty, but as an *internal property*. Yet the impossibility of giving such a definition is obvious, not merely from the failure of all the attempts hitherto made for that purpose, but likewise from the investigation of the sources, from which such a determination ought to be derived.

Although we cannot comprehend, through perception, the objects of those ideas, which, in their nature, lie beyond the world of sense; and though we cannot, on that account, obtain any theoretical intuition of them; we can discover another source, from which, however, we derive no intuitive knowledge of the objects themselves, but a practical and subjective knowledge of their relations to the nature of man. Though our views of the nature of these objects be not thereby enlarged, that knowledge affords us sufficient grounds, upon which we may safely establish rules for our conduct, and convince ourselves of the reality of that ultimate design, which our Reason cannot consistently call in question.

The chief point of this inquiry is, to discover a sufficient ground for the reality of those ideas, and to open a source, from which the determinations of their objects, relative to our practical advantage, shall be derived with safety and without ambiguity. This source, then, according to Kant, lies in the nature of our own subject, i. e. the mind, and is actually that, which we understand by the term *moral sense*. This alone is a safe intuitive ground for determining the reality of the ideas concerning Liberty, God, and Immortality; and this alone establishes the true relations, in which we can form dignified conceptions of the Deity.

KANT

Kant admits it as a matter of fact, that we are moral beings, and consequently this moral sense is an essential part of human nature; that reason places the highest value of man, solely and exclusively, in his moral feelings; and that it reduces all his power and prosperity to these feelings, and values the whole of the former according to effects produced upon the latter. After having demonstrated the essential difference subsisting between the moral and sensitive nature of man, and having analyzed the different laws, by which both are governed respectively; he now proceeds to prove, 1, That the reality of Liberty is necessarily connected with the moral nature of man, and that the latter is wholly inconceivable without the former; that consequently our Reason forces us to acknowledge Liberty as a certain, though unaccountable, fact relative to man; because, without doing this, we would be obliged to renounce all claims to Reason, and to consider it as perfectly useless; 2, That the reality of a being, which contains the sufficient ground of a thorough moral order, must be conceived equally combined with the Deity, as it is with the moral nature of man, so that the immortality of the soul must be considered as a necessary constituent of this moral order. Reason, however, being the supreme tribunal, to which man may appeal, persuades us to receive, not only these ideas, but also their objects as founded upon truth; we are therefore justified in relying upon the justness of our Reason, provided that we do not presume to determine with regard to the internal nature and essence of these objects; a determination, which can be made only through the immediate, though impossible, perception of them. Hence we are utterly incapable of ascertaining the nature of a free subject, as an independent substance; the positive constitution of mind, by which immortality becomes possible; and finally, the manner in which the Deity has accomplished a moral connection between man and the world. We only know, that those objects, which we conceive, through general ideas, as the causes of certain effects, are reclaimed by our reason as the necessary conditions of our moral destination; and that ground, on which we must admit them, or believe their reality, lies in our subject, namely in our moral sense, which partly as an intuitive principle, partly as a practical motive, generates

and

and supports the belief in the fundamental truths of religion. Since, then, the intuitive principle respecting the reality of these transcendental objects, or of religious truths, is perfectly consistent with Reason, not from the immediate perception of objects (the reality of which requires no proof), but from a certain qualification of our own subject, as connected with the real state of these objects; a state, the existence of which is far from being imaginary only; Kant, consequently, calls this a *subjective* ground of conviction, in contradistinction to an *objective* ground, which is derived from the perception of the objects themselves.

In representing the Kantian doctrine of morals, every thing depends upon our being conscious of a moral law, conscious of right and wrong, of good and bad, so that the intuitive ground of moral principles be rendered independent on all theology; for the doctrines of the Deity and Immortality must be deduced from pure morals; or the latter must be the intuitive ground of all religion. And this is likewise the actual and necessary result of his principles. Morality rests upon its own basis; and, in the sublime view which Kant presents of it, all other things relative to man, must be decided by that standard. It is principally in Ethics, we learn, to consider the things of this world as purposes; and by collectively employing them as the means of attaining one ultimate purpose, we introduce unity among them. Thus we discover their subordinate laws, acquire systematic unity, and produce a perfect harmony throughout the whole sphere of the intuitive knowledge of man. Yet, through all the illustrations afforded by Ethics, we do not learn to comprehend the possibility of the things themselves; we only acquire intelligence respecting the possibility of our destination in general. Hence the intuitions, which we derive from morals, do not enlarge our penetration into the nature of the things themselves, but they render our reason consistent with itself, and restore harmony between the moral laws and other intuitions and thoughts; an operation, which is attended with no theoretical, but certainly with great practical, advantage.

This view of morals, however, if it shall serve as the basis of religion, must be extremely different from that, which we find in the " *Systeme de la Nature,* in the writings of HELVETIUS, and several

veral other reputed philosophers, who speak indeed much of Human Nature, but have penetrated less into its essence than they themselves assure us: and though these inquiries constantly appeal to experience, they make use of principles very different from those, which experience *can* furnish.—To describe, at length, the Moral System of Kant, which affords, at once, solidity and consistency in that of Religion, would require a separate publication. But we shall exhibit the outlines of this system in reviewing another work of Kant's, treating particularly of that subject, which the reader will find mentioned under No. XXI. (5) of this analytical retrospect.

XIX. (3) *Prolegomena zu einer jeden künftigen Metaphysik, die als Wissenschaft wird auftreten können.* Introductory observations with respect to every future System of Metaphysics, that may deserve the name of a science. 8vo. *Riga*, 1783, pp. 222.

In the preface to this work, the author explains his aim at convincing those who employ themselves in metaphysical inquiries; that it is indispensably necessary to suspend their labours for some time, to consider every thing hitherto done as undone, and above all things to propose the question, " whether there is any prospect of establishing every where such a science as Metaphysics?"

' If it is a science already, how does it happen, that it has not, like other sciences, obtained general and lasting reputation? If it is none, how is it permitted continually to boast of the illusory name of a science, and to uphold the human understanding with hopes equally permanent and unaccomplished?—Let us therefore demonstrate, either our knowledge or our ignorance; the nature of this pretended science ought to be thoroughly investigated; for it is impossible to leave things any longer upon the old footing. It appears almost ridiculous, while every other science is making incessant progress, that in this one, which aspires to the character of being the oracle of wisdom itself, man continually turns round upon the same spot, without advancing a single step. It is even observed, that the number of its votaries is much decreasing, and that those, who feel themselves sufficiently able to

gain

gain credit in other sciences, do not choose to venture their reputation in this. On the other hand, it is equally certain, that every tyro, who is ignorant in all other branches of knowledge, here claims the right of pronouncing a decisive opinion; because in this territory there exists in fact no settled measure and weight, by which the rational inquirer can be discerned from the shallow prattler.'

'To make plans, is frequently a luxuriant and ostentatious employment of the mind, by which some people acquire the appearance of inventive genius; while they demand what they cannot furnish themselves, censure what they cannot improve, and propose what they themselves do not know where to discover it:—though it may be easily conjectured, that a little more than a declamation of pious wishes will be requisite, to form a just plan of " a general Critique of Reason." But *Pure Reason* is a sphere so insulated and so thoroughly connected with itself, that we can approach no part of it without touching all the rest, and that we can do no good, without having assigned each part its proper place and influence upon the other. For, since without Reason there is nothing that could correct our judgment, the validity and use of every part depends upon the relation, in which it stands towards the others, within the bounds of Reason itself; as in the structure of an organized body the purpose of every member can be deduced only from the complete idea of the whole. Hence we may say of such a *Critique*, that no dependence can be placed upon it, unless it be *entire* and *complete*, even extending to the minutest elements of Pure Reason, and that we must be enabled to determine either *the whole* or *nothing*, that relates to the sphere of this faculty.'

'Although the bare plan of such a science, had it been premised to the " Critique of Pure Reason," might have been unintelligible, suspicious, and useless; it will, on the contrary, become the more advantageous, when it appears in illustration of that work. For, by this plan, we shall be enabled to take a view of the whole, to investigate the principal points, upon the solidity of which this science is erected, and to understand more clearly the principles, which at first appeared obscure.'

'These Prolegomena then contain such a plan as ought to be stated

stated in an analytical method, since the preceding work necessarily required a synthethical arrangement: in order that this science might be exhibited in its individual parts, and as the structure of a very peculiar faculty in the acquisition of knowledge, which presents itself in its natural connection. Those who should find this plan as obscure as the Critique itself, must consider that the study of Metaphysics is not the business of all; that there are many ingenious men, who make considerable proficiency in sciences, that lie more within the bounds of sensible perception, and who do not succeed in inquiries carried on through pure abstract notions. Such individuals must employ their mental faculties upon other objects. Those, however, who venture to judge upon Metaphysics, or even attempt to frame systems of their own, must previously satisfy the demands made in this work. Whether this be done by approving of the method, in which I have solved the different problems; or by refuting this solution, upon well established principles, and giving another in its place; in either case they will do justice to the cause. For, to reject a plan without trying its merits, is equally frivolous and illiberal. I confess I did not expect to hear philosophers complaining, that my works were deficient in popular, entertaining, and easy language; when the question relates to the existence of a source of knowledge, which is highly valuable and indispensable to man, but which cannot be demonstrated, without observing the strictest rules of scientific deduction. Popularity, indeed, will in its turn attend these investigations, but to aim at it in the beginning, would be a silly and fruitless attempt.—That very obscurity, which is so much decried, and which is frequently used as a cloak for the conveniency and mental weakness of its adversaries, is not without relative advantage; for all those, who observe a cautious silence in other sciences, enjoy an opportunity of speaking and deciding in a magisterial tone upon metaphysical subjects; because their ignorance, here, does not form so remarkable a contrast, when compared with the knowledge of others, as it does in opposition to genuine critical principles, of which we may justly say with the Roman poet,

Ignavum, fucos, pecus a præsepibus arcent.'
VIRG.

As these Prolegomena are a concise and perspicuous abstract from the preceding *Critique*, in an analytical method, which the author employs, as it were, to go back again the same path, upon which he had synthetically advanced in the Critique; we could only repeat that deduction of Kant's principles, which we have already premised at sufficient length.

XX. (4.) *Betrachtungen über das Fundament der Kräfte und Methoden, welche die Vernunft anwenden kann, darüber zu urtheilen.* Reflections upon the foundation of the powers and methods, which Reason is entitled to employ in judging upon their validity. 8vo. *Koenigsberg,* 1784.

Of this small work, I know little more than its title, not having been able to procure a copy of it; and as, from the German Reviews, it appears to be a further deduction of the principles laid down in the preceding two works, I shall immediately, and at considerable length, review the following, which is uniformly considered as the most perspicuous and valuable production of Kant.

XXI. (5) *Grundlegung zur Metaphysik der Sitten.* Fundamental principles of the Metaphysicks (Theory) of Morals. 8vo. *Riga.* 1785.—2d Edit. 1792, pp. 128 and 14 pp. Preface.

The outlines of KANT's System of Morals, I shall endeavour to exhibit, as clearly as possible, in the following analysis of his principles.

The desire of happiness is inherent in human nature: all the instinctive propensities of man are directed to that purpose. But our reason still restrains that desire, and considers only such a possession of happiness as worthy of our exertions, which is perfectly consistent with morality, or rather, which is the reward of moral actions. Morality and happiness, therefore, are two different but essential determinations originating in human nature; which, when united by the dictates of reason, render the destination of man perfect. This union, however, cannot be better conceived by reason, than that morality itself contains the cause, through which the happiness of man is accomplished. If we ourselves are the purposes and not the *bare* means in the hands of nature or any other Being; it follows, that the necessary attributes of our constitution must likewise be conceived as possible: there must exist such an arrangement of things, as contributes to realize our moral destination. The former part of this destination, namely morality, depends on ourselves, and on the degree of self-activity, with which we practise the moral law. This faculty of practising what the moral law commands, we presuppose in every rational being; for otherwise it would be highly absurd, to impose upon ourselves a law, obedience to which Reason could not acknowledge as practicable. It must consequently be in our power, to be morally good, if Reason commands us to act in conformity to the moral law. In whatever subject then Reason actually exists, it must also be possible, that it manifest itself by actions: whoever has the ability to apprehend what is good as a thing absolutely necessary, on its own account, he must likewise be provided with the faculty of performing it. But it is not physically necessary to do it; for we nowhere discover our Reason subject to this species of necessity. Why Reason very frequently does not practise what it must acknowledge to be morally good; why our sensitive nature is not always vanquished, but frequently prevails in this contest; these problems we are unable to solve; because we do not in any manner comprehend that, which forms the moral nature of man, as an object of perception; and because we can only derive the moral faculty of man from the idea of the possibility of morality in general. We know only this much with certainty, that we judge upon the moral value of man, merely and entirely, by the degree of moral motives, which we observe in his actions or sentiments. If, therefore, the physical energy is properly arranged in a man, so that the use of Reason, in general, is possible to him; we presuppose, that the performance of morally good actions is really entrusted to his will: and if we did not presuppose this inclination, we would in fact deny all the influence which Reason exercises over human affairs, and thus be obliged to declare the general laws of morality, afforded by this faculty, as mere phantoms of the brain. Our moral perfection depends upon our own exertions, and it is from this quarter, that we may more and more approach our destination.

What

What, on the other hand, relates to the second part of our destination, namely to our happiness; this depends on the institution of the things in nature, as well those of our own subject as the external objects, and their influence upon us. By means of Reason and its inherent liberty, we can indeed make such a use of the things in nature, as to produce certain degrees or parts of happiness. But the rules calculated to produce these effects, Reason cannot derive from its own nature *a priori*, as is the case with the moral law; because experience must be consulted first, that we may learn, how the nature of man, and that of individual subjects, is constituted, and in what relation the things are to human happiness. The laws by which happiness is attained, are founded upon the nature of phenomena: man may apply them to his advantage, but he cannot determine them; he may regulate, in a certain degree, the influence of the things upon himself; but he must still submit to their laws. If, then, we were to consult Reason, and to ask, by what laws happiness ought to be distributed in the world; it could give no other answer, but that the moral law ought to decide this. Morality should always be attended with a proportionate share of happiness; whether it of itself produced that happiness as its real cause (according to physical influence), or that a third being allotted to every individual, such a portion of happiness as he deserved through the degree of his moral activity:—here we would admit an *ideal* influence, in which a third being had so regulated the course of nature, that her laws were in perfect harmony with the demands of Reason, relative to the happiness of moral beings.

But if we consult experience, we by no means learn, that such a moral order really subsists in the world; since we frequently observe men of bad morals, and of a depraved character, apparently happy, while good and virtuous men are afflicted by misfortunes. For, though the consciousness of just and good actions be accompanied with agreeable feelings, this alone does not constitute human happiness; since the most excellent man must be called unhappy, if he is labouring under such calamities as are the permanent cause of painful sensations. The wants of human nature are very numerous! Many of them are independent on our will: the failure in satisfying urgent necessities, is unavoidably accompanied with pain, frequently the most acute; nay, even a great number of the voluntary or artificial wants are, by degrees and through incidental circumstances, so intimately interwoven with the well-being of man, that he must always feel unhappy, when he is deprived of those means, by which he was accustomed to satisfy them. Besides, there is a great number of accidents, which render him who is exposed to them always unhappy; and experience does not teach us, that any distinction prevails here between the good and bad. Diseases, war, famine, and all physical evils, oppress the honest man with equal, and frequently with much greater, rigour than the dishonest: the former, as well as the latter, is placed in unhappy situations, without the means of evading these evils. It requires, upon the whole, no proof that in the distribution of physical goods, though a necessary part of human happiness, no moral order at all can be discovered in experience; and that, if the latter alone could decide the question, we must explain all the agreement between happiness and virtue, entirely by the law of chance. What happens in nature according to physical laws, is equally different from what ought to happen according to the laws of moral order, as the usual actions of man differ from their duties.

But although we observe in this world no such moral order, as exhibits happiness and morality in constant proportion; our Reason still preserves an uncommon propensity to maintain, that such an order must actually exist. This, however, is a presupposition, which can be justified, neither by argument nor demonstration, nor through the real exposition of such an order; but which is established merely upon a ground contained in our own mind. This ground rests on the necessary internal obligation of being morally good, or on the moral feelings common to all mankind, and acknowledged by all good men. The actual existence of a moral order is so intimately connected with these feelings, that the consciousness of them continually impels us to presuppose this order. And the more eagerly we cultivate morality, by displaying much vigour in the observation of its laws; the more firmly and thoroughly we become convinced, that there must exist a complete moral order.

The

The train of thought, by which Reason forms and justifies this conclusion, is nearly the following.

Reason acknowledges it as indispensably necessary, that man ought to act conformably to moral laws. As long as man enjoys the use of Reason, no situation or relation in life can be conceived, in which he is exempted from the obligation of acting as a moral being. To act morally right, is therefore the highest object, at which every man ought to aim: Reason cannot, upon any condition whatever, reverse this judgment, without falling into an obvious contradiction with itself. Now, we find, in human nature, at the same time, a desire of happiness, which is not always gratified. Our nature, however, is so constituted, that we must feel a necessary desire of happiness; and this natural wish is a sufficient ground for exerting ourselves, to realize it by all the means in our power. The rules, in consequence of which men attain to real happiness, are solely and exclusively learned from experience; while the moral laws are derived *a priori* from Reason: and thus it happens, that many rules for procuring happiness are contrary to morality; or that they weaken the force of the moral law. Nevertheless, Reason places a much higher value on morality, and commands us to wish for no other happiness, but such as is in perfect harmony with moral feelings. Upon this very occasion we learn, that the happiness of men is connected with conditions and circumstances, so various and incidental, that we cannot always attain it, by practising either the laws of morality or prudence. For, the moral conduct does not, as far as experience informs us, necessarily produce happiness; since we observe no physical connection between them; and since the association of good fortune with a moral conduct appears to be merely accidental. Even the utmost prudence of man cannot rear the fabric of felicity, though he should act in defiance of morality, and endeavour to make happiness his only and unconditional object. For the latter depends on too many circumstances, over which man has no power of controul, and through which frequently the wisest plans may be rendered abortive.

The happiness of a moral being, in a moral order of things, can properly be said to consist in no other maxim than the following:

" every

"every thing that happens, is in strict harmony with the general laws of morality." Even the good man can wish and desire nothing further. If he now admit a moral principle or a God, he must likewise expect, that every thing shall really correspond with moral purposes; and consequently, if a man act virtuously, he can expect nothing else, in a moral world, but real happiness. In fact, therefore, man awaits his prosperity from good fortune, the dispensation of which is entrusted to a wise Providence. This hope is entirely supported by the belief in God, and it is equally constant and safe as the latter.

Since man possesses no power over all those things, which relate to his ultimate destination, no other condition of attaining this remains for the virtuous, but to consider the whole world subject to a moral order; that is, to look upon moral beings as absolute and ultimate purposes, to which every thing relates, that is real in the world; or to consider these beings as containing the cause, on account of which every thing is thus constituted, and not otherwise. For, if these contain the ground of the constitution of the world, there must exist a certain order in it, conformably to which the essential purposes of moral beings can be attained. Allowing, therefore, that happiness is a part of the essential destination of human nature, and that men themselves belong to the class of moral beings; nature itself must be so constituted, that their happiness can be effected by her aid. But the destination of human nature is not completed by the attainment of that happiness alone, which consists in mere enjoyment, but by morality, in union with happiness, and indeed so modified, that the latter be in proportion to the former. Morality must determine the measure of happiness allotted to every individual, and not *vice versa*. If thus we shall conceive the attainment of our destination, as a possible event; we must admit a thorough moral order as really subsisting, though it be not in our power to produce an *objective* proof of it. The ground, on which we admit it, lies merely in our own mind, and indeed in the conviction, that we are moral beings designed for ultimate purposes. To conceive these beings in connection with other things, is altogether impossible, unless we grant, that the latter relate to the former, and facilitate the attainment

tainment of their destination. It is, consequently, the reflection made upon our own moral nature, which induces us to admit the existence of a moral order.

Though we cannot discover this moral order in experience, the truth of it is not thereby in the least degree affected, nor can it be disputed from that source. For experience could no where prove the existence of a thorough moral order, although all the phenomena, that we observe, should correspond with the idea of it. It would ever remain doubtful, whether this correspondence be general and constant, unless a very different manner of representing it, afforded certainty to the conclusions thus arising. For, to comprehend the reality of such an order *a posteriori*, there would be required a complete view of all things and their relations to one another; a view, that is unattainable by beings so constituted as we are. And the circumstance of our finding virtue frequently accompanied by misfortune, is by no means inconsistent with the *idea* of a moral order. This idea does not imply the necessity, that every moral action shall be immediately attended with a certain portion of happiness, or that the latter be physically produced: it involves only this much, that the lot of man, upon the whole, is in a certain harmony with his moral character. In this way it is not difficult to conceive, that one or several periods of his existence are particularly designed for the purpose of improving his moral nature, and that good and bad fortune may be so distributed during these periods, that they can be used rather as the means of improvement, than to serve as the scale of ascertaining the moral excellence of the individual. Nevertheless, the regulations in the world may be so made, that such a share of happiness arises from them for each moral being, as it has merited by its conduct. We elevate man above the consideration of his being a passive instrument in the hands of nature, when we represent him as sacrificing a part of that happiness, of which his sensitive nature is susceptible; in order to contribute his share, that other rational beings may likewise attain their destination; provided that he does not neglect his own. For, Reason itself must approve of such a regulation. If now, from this point of view, we consider the events and the vicissitudes of human life, which we observe by experience in the world of sense; all the facts thus obtained are perfectly consistent with the possibility of a moral order. We must however not attempt to make such use of them, as if they were absolute proofs; since they can be used only as arguments for disproving the contrary of a moral order. But if we represent the question upon this foundation, that moral actions *ought* to produce happiness conformably to the laws of nature; then the instances, by which we prove that virtue and misfortune are in certain cases accompanied by one another, would not only be irrefutable, but they would likewise prove the nullity of this complete moral order.

In the Kantian philosophy, it is a matter of no importance, and wholly undetermined, *how* such an order is *really* possible. The reality of it, KANT does not attempt to demonstrate from a pretended view of its causes; he rather grants, that these are to us altogether inconceivable. He only admits this moral order, on account of the strong and constant demands of Reason; a faculty, that thinks or judges of moral beings as absolute and ultimate, to whom every thing else relates, and who consequently must determine the order of all other things, and their relations to the moral beings themselves.

Thus we presuppose a moral order, while we confidently rely upon our Reason and our moral nature; because the reality of it must be conceived from its being so intimately united with our moral feelings. It is certain, that we are moral agents, consequently the conditions must also be certain, without which our moral nature, in the eyes of our own Reason, would be a nonentity. According to Reason, however, our moral nature consists in this, that man is an absolute purpose, to which all other things are subordinate means. Yet morality and happiness, united to one purpose, compose the destination of man, so that the former determines the latter. Without a moral order, this is impossible. And as, agreeably to Reason, moral beings must have it in their power to contribute towards the attainment of their destination; the reality of a moral order must likewise be admitted; because it is the only condition, upon which this inference can be justified. If we then allow the existence of a moral order, we must also submit to those conditions, without which it is wholly impossible. Though we cannot

cannot comprehend the real possibility of this order, we must nevertheless grant, that those conditions are real, without which such an order cannot at all be conceived. But it is inconceivable, if we do not admit, 1, that the laws of the world of sense are not the only ones, by which all events are determined; that the world itself is subject to still higher laws, and upon the whole, relates to something, which is independent on the world, or external to it, and to which the world is merely subservient; 2, that there exists a cause, through which every thing is determined according to the laws of a moral order, to which consequently every thing is subject, and upon which every thing in the world depends; and lastly, 3, that the personality or individual existence of man continues, in order that through him the moral order may be accomplished.

It is easy to perceive, that the first of these postulates leads to the idea of a supersensible world, which is independent on the laws subsisting in the world of sense, i. e. which is *free*. The second idea involves the conception of a *Deity*. For, if we separate every arbitrary and adventitious matter from the idea of the Deity, and preserve that alone, upon which a representation worthy of so sublime a Being can be established; nothing further remains than the thought of a connection or relation, by means of which that Being must be the foundation of a thorough moral order. No other idea, however, but that of an intelligent power could entitle or even induce us to entertain a notion like that of moral order; hence it is conceivable, how in this idea alone we meet with some analogy, that serves to distinguish so sublime a Being, and, together with the most perfect will, to attribute to it all those properties, through which only so sacred a will can be exerted. Lastly; that the third principle before stated, leads to the *Immortality of the soul*, is now a very rational inference.

The idea of *Liberty*, or the faculty of determining our actions uninfluenced by sensual motives, and self active, through the consciousness of the moral law alone; this idea is involved in that of morality. We therefore undoubtedly possess that liberty, as we are moral agents; and the conception of liberty in general has been perfectly justified by showing, that the physical world is not the only one, which influences the nature of man; that it is connected with beings of a very different kind, whose actions are determined by very different laws. The idea of a moral order stands in the same relation to that of our being moral agents, whose destination is certainly attainable; as the former is connected with the idea of God and Immortality; so that if we admit the truth of the one, the relation of the others must likewise be granted. Thus we are sufficiently and perfectly authorized to believe in God and Immortality, as the two essential pillars of all Religion; though the arguments for this belief, are not taken from the perception of objects, but are derived from the more permanent nature of our mind.

Upon a cursory view of the statement here given, it might perhaps appear to some readers, as if in Kant's process of reasoning, first morality is represented as the ground-work of Religion, and afterwards Religion again is called an aid, to support the idea of a moral law. But, upon a mature consideration of the subject, this appearance will very soon vanish. For, the ground of discovering a moral law, lies merely and exclusively in our Reason, which presents to us this law, as soon as it is conceived in a practical or active sense; and which, independent on all Religion, imposes upon us the obligation of observing the precepts of morality. But if, with this moral obligation, we compare nature and her relations to the destination of man, Reason requires, that nature should likewise agree with the destination of moral beings; because, in the contrary case, that value which Reason places upon its faculties and operations, and which is to be computed much higher than Nature itself, would not be real, but altogether imaginary. Thus convinced of a moral order, man may certainly make use of it, in order to remove those difficulties, which present themselves in the practice of the moral law. The doubts and uncertainties, which may arise against the reality of a moral order of things, are thereby suppressed; the sensual appetites, too, are through this conviction so modified and regulated, that they shall be indulged only with a view of such an happiness as is consistent with virtue, while they gradually become familiar with the order, that is manifest throughout all nature. Besides, this mode of representing a

system

syſtem contains a great number of arguments, from which even the ſenſitive faculty derives ſome conſolation, if its purpoſes ſhould be occaſionally defeated, and its neceſſities too much limited; for there ſtill remains a ſtate, in which this alſo may be ſatisfied; provided that man perſeveres in obeying the dictates of morality. Thus Religion certainly contains arguments in favour of morality, and on this very account it is calculated to remove many obſtacles, which may occur in the practice of the moral law. Religion, therefore, offers no intuitive ground of diſcovering moral precepts, though it can be employed as an excellent pſychological aid of ſtrengthening the moral faculty of human nature; ſince it overcomes thoſe difficulties, which frequently ariſe from falſe reflections, and which obſtruct the due exerciſe of that faculty.

XXII. (6) *Metaphyſiſche Anfangsgründe der Naturwiſſenſchaft*. Metaphyſical Principles of Natural Philoſophy. 8vo. *Riga*, 1786. 2d Edit. 1787, pp. 158, and xxiv pages Preface.

This is, without exception, the moſt profound of KANT's works; and in order to afford the reader a conciſe view of the author's aim, I ſhall firſt give an abſtract from the elaborate Preface to this publication, and then exhibit the principles of this *new* ſcience, in a cloſe tranſlation.

' It is of the greateſt importance to the progreſs of the ſciences, " ſays Kant," to ſeparate diſſimilar principles from one another, to reduce each ſet of them to a particular ſyſtem, that they may form a ſcience of a peculiar kind. Thus we ſhall prevent that uncertainty in ſciences, which ariſes from confounding them, and in conſequence of which we cannot eaſily diſtinguiſh the limits, which, in a doubtful caſe, are to be aſſigned to each of them; nor can we diſcover the ſource of the errors, that may attend the practical application of them. On this account, I have deemed it neceſſary, to exhibit ſyſtematically the *pure* part of Natural Philoſophy (*Phyſica generalis*), in which metaphyſical and mathematical conſtructions of ideas occur promiſcuouſly; and, in treating of the former, to ſhow at the ſame time the principles of that conſtruction,

and

and consequently to prove the possibility of a System of Natural Philosophy, deduced from mathematical demonstrations. This division of sciences, beside the advantage already stated, is attended with the particular satisfaction, which the unity and harmony of knowledge afford, when we can prevent the limits of the sciences from interfering with one another.'

' As a second reason of recommending this process, it may be urged, that in every department of Metaphysics we may hope to attain to *absolute completeness*, such as we cannot expect in any other species of knowledge; consequently, the completeness of the Metaphysics of material nature may be expected, here, with the same confidence as in the Metaphysics of nature in general. For, in Metaphysics, the object is merely considered, agreeably to the general laws of thought, while in other sciences it must be represented according to the different data of perception, whether this be pure or empirical. In Metaphysics, too, we acquire a determined number of cognitions, which can be completely exhausted; because, here, the object must be continually compared with all the necessary laws of thought: while in the other sciences, on account of the infinite variety of perceptions, or objects of thought, which they present to the mind, we never can attain to absolute completeness, but may extend them in infinitum, as is the case with pure Mathematics and experimental Physics. I likewise believe, that I have completely stated these metaphysical principles of Natural Philosophy, to their utmost extent; but though I have succeeded in this attempt, I do not flatter myself with having performed any extraordinary task.'

' To complete, however, a metaphysical system, whether that of nature in general, or that of the material world, the Table of the Categories * must serve as its Schema. For there are in reality no more nor fewer pure intellectual notions concerning the nature of things, than I have stated in that Table. All the determinations relative to the general notion of matter, consequently all that can be conceived of it *a priori*, that can be exhibited in mathematical construction, or that can be proposed as a determined object of experience, must admit of being reduced to the

four

---

* Vid. the *Categories*, p. 45, and their *Schemata*, p. 47.

four classes of the Categories, viz. that of Quantity, Quality, Relation, and Modality. There remains nothing to be discovered or added here; but if imperfections should occur, with respect to perspicuity and order, the system in this respect may be occasionally improved.'

'The idea of matter must, therefore, be examined through all the four mentioned functions of the intellect (in four Sections), in each of which a new determination of that idea occurs. The primary attribute of something, that represents an object of the external senses, must be motion; for by that only can these senses be affected. To this, the Understanding reduces all other predicates of matter, that relate to its nature; and thus Natural Philosophy is, throughout, either a pure or applied *theory of motion*. The metaphysical principles of this science must, consequently, be divided into four Sections: in the *first* of which, motion is considered as a pure quantum, according to its composition, without any quality of that which is moveable, and hence may be called PHORONOMY; in the *second*, motion is investigated in its relation to the quantity of matter, under the name of an originally moving power, and is therefore called DYNAMICS; in the *third*, matter is examined in reciprocal relation to this quantity, by its peculiar motion, and appears under the title of MECHANICS; and in the *fourth* Section, the motion or rest of matter is determined merely in relation to the mode of representing it, or *Modality*, consequently as phenomenon of external senses, on which account is is called PHENOMENOLOGY.'

CONTENTS.

SECT. I. *Metaphysical principles of* PHORONOMY.

POSITION 1. Matter is that which is *moveable* in space. That space, which itself is moveable, is called the *material*, or likewise, *relative space*; that, in which all *motion* must be ultimately conceived (and which consequently in its own nature is absolutely immoveable), is called the pure, or likewise, *absolute space*.

Posit. 2. The motion of a thing is the change of its *external relations* to given space.

Posit. 3. *Rest* is the permanent presence (*præsentia perdurabilis*) in the same place; *permanent* however is that which exists, i. e. continues for a certain time.

Posit. 4. To *construct* the idea of compound motion, means to represent motion a priori in the perceptive faculty, as far as the former arises from two or several joint motions in one moveable space.

Theorem. Every motion, as object of experience, may be considered, either as the motion of a body in a resting space, or as the rest of a body and, on the other hand, motion of space in opposite direction with equal velocity.

Posit. 5. The *combination* of *motion* is the representation of the motion of a point, as being homologous with two or several motions of it united together.

SECT. II. *Metaphysical principles of* DYNAMICS.

Posit. 1. *Matter* is that which is *moveable*, so far as it *fills a space*. To *fill* a space, is to resist all that is moveable and that makes an effort, by its motion, to penetrate into a certain space. A space that is not filled, is a *vacuum*.

Theorem, 1. Matter fills a space, not by its mere *existence*, but by a particular *moving power.*

Posit. 2. The *power* of *attraction* is that moving power, by which one matter may be the cause of the approach of others towards it; or, in other words, by which it resists the removal of others from it.—The *power of repulsion* is that, by which one matter may be the cause of removing others from it ; or, in other words, by which it resists the approach of others towards it.

Theorem 2d. Matter fills its spaces by the repulsive power of all its parts, i. e. by a peculiar power of extension, that has a determined degree, beyond which smaller or greater degrees may be conceived in infinitum.

Posit 3. One matter, in its motion, *penetrates* another, when, by means of compression, it completely removes the space of its extension.

Theorem 3d. Matter may be *compressed* in infinitum, but it never can be *penetrated* by matter, however great its pressing power may be.

Posit.

Posit. 4. That *impenetrability* of matter, which depends upon the resistance proportionally increasing with the degrees of compression, is called *relative*; as on the contrary that, which rests upon the *supposition*, that matter, as such, is not liable to any compression whatever, is here called *absolute* impenetrability.—The *filling* of *space* with absolute impenetrability may be called *mathematical*, while that of relative impenetrability receives the name of *dynamical*.

Posit. 5. *Material substance* is that in space, which is moveable of itself, i. e. separate from every other thing that exists without it in space. The motion of a part of matter, by which it ceases to be a part, is *separation*. The separation of the parts of matter is the *physical division*.

Theorem 4th. Matter is *divisible in infinitum*, and indeed into parts, each of which is again matter.

Theorem. 5th. The possibility of matter renders a power of attraction necessary; this being the second essential and fundamental power of it.

Theorem 6th. By the mere power of attraction, without that of repulsion, we cannot conceive the possibility of any matter.

Posit. 6. Contact, in a physical sense, is immediate action and reaction of *impenetrability*. The action of one matter upon another, without contact, is the *action at distance* (*actio in distans*). This action at distance, which is possible even without the aid of intervenient matter, is called the immediate *action* of matter upon matter, *through empty space*.

Theorem 7th. The *attraction essential to all matter*, is the immediate action of it upon another matter, through empty space.

Posit. 7th. A moving power, by which matters can immediately act upon one another only in a common surface of contact, is called a *superficial power*; but that, by which one matter can immediately act upon the parts of another, even beyond the surface of contact, may be called a *penetrating power*.

Theorem 8th. The original power of attraction, upon which the possibility of matter itself, as such, must depend, extends in the universe immediately from every part of it to another *ad infinitum*.

SECT III. *Metaphysical principles of* MECHANICS.

Posit. 1. *Matter* is that which is *moveable*, so far as it (as such) possesses moving power.

Posit. 2. The *quantity of matter* is the amount of that which is moveable in a determined space. This, so far as all its parts are considered in their motions as operating (moving) at the same time, is called *congeries*; and we say, that a matter acts in a congeries, when all its parts, moved in the same direction, exercise their moving power externally, and *at the same time*. A congeries consisting of a determined shape is called a *body* (in a mechanical sense). The *magnitude* of *motion* (mechanically computed) is that which is estimated both by the quantity of matter moved, and its velocity: when *phoronomically* considered, it consists merely in the degree of velocity.

Theorem 1st. The quantity of a piece of matter, in comparison with *any* other, can be estimated only by the quantity of motion in a given velocity.

Theorem 2d. *First law of Mechanics.* In all the changes of corporeal nature, the quantity of matter remains, upon the whole, without increasing or diminishing.

Theorem 3d. *Second law of Mechanics.* Every change of matter has an external cause. (Every material body remains in its state of rest or motion, in the same direction, and with the same velocity, unless it be compelled by some external cause, to change this state.)

Theorem 4th. *Third Mechanical law.* In every communicated motion, the action and reaction always correspond with one another.

SECT. IV. *Metaphysical principles of* PHENOMENOLOGY.

Posit. *Matter* is that which is *moveable*, as far as in that respect it can be an object of experience.

Theorem 1st. The motion of matter, in a straight line, is, with respect to an empirical space, merely a *possible* predicate, in contradistinction to the opposite motion of space. The very same predicate

predicate is *impossible*, if we conceive it in no external relation to matter, i. e. as *absolute motion*.

Theorem 2d. The circular motion of matter, in contradistinction to the opposite motion of space, is a *real* predicate of it; whereas the opposite motion of a relative space, if substituted for the motion of the body, is no real motion of the latter, and if considered as such, is a mere illusion.

Theorem 3d. In every motion of a body, by which it is moving, with respect to another body, an opposite equal motion of the latter is *necessary*.

XXIII. (7) *Grundlegung zur Critik des Geschmacks*. Fundamental principles of the Critique of Taste. 8vo. *Riga*. 1787.

Though we have not succeeded in procuring a copy of this publication, we shall find an opportunity of stating the outlines of Kant's ideas upon this interesting subject, in a subsequent work, under No. XXV. (9), in which he considers the various *judgments* resulting from *Taste*; the modes, in which they take place in the mind; and their respective peculiarities.

XXIV. (8.) *Critik der practischen Vernunft*. Critique of Practical Reason. 8vo. *Riga*. 1788. 2d Edit. 1792.

If we abstract from the *empirical* part of experience, or if we conceive experience as a general idea, without attending to any variety that may be contained under this idea; we then acquire *a priori* the conditions of it. The empirical or experimental knowledge obtained by experience formed the *matter* of it; but those conditions, without which experience cannot be reduced to the rules of thought, we have called the *form* of it.—We must proceed in a similar manner, when we reflect upon the various operations of our *will*. I will, for instance, any one object, and I immediately become conscious of the idea relating to some expected pleasure; an idea, which is connected with this will. The representation of that pleasure, which the possession of the object might afford, is the empirical part of the will, that constitutes its matter. If we abstract from the latter, there is produced the idea of a *free will*, the condition as it were of every thing that is empirical. If, further, we lay aside in thought every thing that refers to experience, and still suppose a will completely determined towards acting; there remains at last nothing but the faculty of reason itself, which determines this will to act. In this manner arises in us the idea of a *Practical Reason*; a faculty, which directs the will, independent of any impulse of the senses. The " Critique of Practical Reason," therefore, sets out with the design of investigating this faculty.

CONTENTS.

BOOK I. ANALYSIS OF PURE PRACTICAL REASON.

SECT. I. *Of the principles of pure practical Reason.*

Illustration. Practical *principles* are such as contain a general determination of the will, which again has a variety of subordinate practical rules. They are subjective principles or *maxims*, when the condition is considered as applicable only to the will of the subject; but they are *objective* principles or practical *laws*, when that condition is acknowledged as objective, i. e. applicable to the will of every rational being.

Theorem 1st. All practical principles, which presuppose an *object* (matter) of the desiring faculty as the cause of determining the will, are wholly empirical, and cannot furnish practical laws.

Theorem 2d. All the practical principles relating to material objects, are, as such, without exception, of one and the same kind, and originate from the general principle of self-love or personal happiness.

Theorem 3d. If a rational being shall conceive its maxims as practical general laws; it can consider them only as principles, which contain the ground of determining the will, not according to the matter, but merely according to the form.

Fundamental law of pure practical Reason.

" Let such be your conduct, that the maxim of your will
" may, in every instance, be admitted as the principle of a
" general law;—or in other words:
" Act in such a manner, as to consider and to employ hu-
" manity,

" manity, in your own as well as in every other perſon, al-
" ways as the *purpoſe*, but never as the *means* of obtaining your
" object."

Theorem 4th. The *autonomy* of the will is the only principle of all moral laws, and of the duties conformable to them: all *heteronomy* of choice, therefore, not only eſtabliſhes no obligation whatever, but is likewiſe contrary to the principles of it, and to the moral purity of the will. The ſole principle of morality conſiſts in the independence, namely of all matter of the law (i. e. the object deſired), and at the ſame time in the determination of the choice by the pure general legiſlative forms, of which a maxim muſt be ſuſceptible. That *independence*, however, is liberty in a *negative* ſenſe; whereas this *peculiar legiſlative power* of pure, and as ſuch practical, Reaſon is liberty in a *poſitive* ſenſe. Hence the moral law expreſſes nothing elſe but the *autonomy* of pure practical Reaſon, i. e. of liberty, and this itſelf is the formal condition of all maxims, under which alone they can correſpond with the ſupreme practical law. If, therefore, the matter of volition, which can be nothing elſe but the object of a deſire that is connected with the law, enters into the *condition of its poſſibility*; there ariſes from it the heteronomy of choice, namely, the dependence on the law of nature, to follow any one impulſe or inclination; and the will does not give itſelf the law, but only the precept for a rational obſervance of pathological laws. But the maxim, which in this way never can contain the general legiſlative form, upon the ſame ground eſtabliſhes not only no obligation, but is likewiſe contrary to the principle of a *pure* practical Reaſon, conſequently alſo to moral ſentiment, although the action thus ariſing ſhould be lawful.

SECT II. *Of the idea concerning the object of pure practical Reaſon.*

TABLE

Of the Categories of Liberty relative to the cognitions we poſſeſs of the Good and Bad.

1.
Of Quantity.

Subjective, in consequence of maxims: (*opinions depending upon the will* of the individual;)
Objective, in consequence of principles: (*precepts*;)
A priori objective as well as *subjective* principles of liberty; (*laws.*)

2.
Of Quality:

practical rules of *appetition*, (*præceptivæ*,)
practical rules of *omission*, (*prohibitivæ*,)
practical rules of *exceptions*, (*exceptivæ*.)

3.
Of Relation:

To *personality*,
To the *condition* of the person,
Reciprocally of one person to the condition of another.

4.
Of Modality;

Permitted and *nonpermitted* actions,
Duty and contrary to duty,
perfect and *imperfect* duty.

SECT. III. *Of the motives of pure practical Reason.*
   Critical illustration of the analysis of pure practical Reason.

BOOK II. DIALECTIC OF PURE PRACTICAL REASON.

I. Antinomy of pure practical Reason.
II. Critical solution of this antinomy.
III. Of the principal advantage of pure practical Reason, in its connection with the speculative.
IV. On the immortality of the soul, as a postulate of pure practical Reason.
V. On the existence of a God, as a similar postulate.
VI. On the postulates of pure practical Reason in general.
VII. In what manner an extensive improvement of pure practical Reason

Reason is conceivable in a particular view, without increasing at the same time its speculative knowledge.

VIII. Of supposed truths, being a necessary result of pure Reason.

IX. Of the cognoscible faculties of man, being wisely proportioned to his practical destination.

Methodical doctrine of pure practical Reason.

XXV. (9) *Critik der Urtheilskraft.*—Critique of the Judging Faculty. 8vo. *Libau*, 1790. 2d Edit. *Berlin.* 1793, pp. 482, and lxx pp. Preface and Introduction.

The author's principal aim in this work is to inquire, ' whether the *Judging Faculty*, which, in the order of our cognoscible powers, forms an intermediate capacity between the Understanding and Reason, has likewise its own principles *a priori*; whether these are constitutive or merely regulative; and whether that faculty of judging affords *a priori* the rule for the sensations of pleasure and displeasure, which again are the intermediate degrees between the cognoscible and appetitive faculties.'

' A Critique of pure Reason, i. e. of our capacity of judging conformably to principles *a priori*, would be incomplete, if the Judging Faculty, which likewise claims these principles, were not treated as a separate part of that Critique; although, in a system of pure philosophy, the principles of judgment must not be considered as a separate part, belonging either to the theoretical or practical department of the system; but, in cases of emergency, they may be occasionally connected with either. For, if such a system shall once be established under the general name of Metaphysics (a work, the complete attainment of which is by no means impossible, and which would be of the first importance to the general use of Reason); the Critique must have previously investigated the ground, on which this structure is to be erected, as well as the solidity of the basis of this faculty, that deduces its principles independent on experience: and if any one part of this fabric should be found to stand upon a slight foundation, the downfal of the whole would be the inevitable consequence.

' But we may easily perceive from the nature of the Judging Faculty, that the discovery of the peculiar principle of it, must be

attended

attended with great difficulties; for this faculty must necessarily contain some such principle *a priori*; because, in the contrary case, it could not be subject to the most common critique as a particular faculty of acquiring knowledge; and because the proper use of it is so necessary, and so universally admitted, that every body is acquainted with its influence. That principle, however, must not be derived from notions *a priori*, since these are the property of the Understanding, and the application of them only belongs to the Judging Faculty. Hence the latter must furnish an idea, through which indeed we obtain no intuition of any object, but which serves as a rule to that faculty itself. This rule, however, is not of an *objective* nature, so that we could compare the judgment with it *in concreto*; for to do this, there would be required a second Judging Faculty, in order to enable us to distinguish, whether the case applies to the rule or not.

' This perplexity on account of a principle (whether a subjective or objective one) chiefly manifests itself in those judgments which are called *aesthetical*, which relate to the Beautiful and the Sublime, whether that of nature or art. And yet is the critical investigation of a principle of the Judging Faculty, respecting those objects, the most important part of the Critique of this power. For, though the aesthetical judgments, of themselves, contribute nothing to the knowledge we obtain of things, they nevertheless belong exclusively to the cognoscible faculty, and evince the immediate relation of this faculty to the sensations of pleasure and displeasure, in consequence of some one principle a priori, without confounding it with that, which may be the cause of determining the appetitive faculty; because this has its principles a priori in notions, which are the produce of Reason.'

Having premised this extract from the author's preface to the work under consideration, I shall only add the result of KANT's inquiry respecting the final purposes of nature, as exhibited in the SECOND BOOK of this publication; though, in my opinion, this investigation forms the most interesting and essential part of the whole. It is as follows.

In conformity to our Reason, we are obliged to assume a certain connection, subsisting between the final purposes of nature, in the manner as our Understanding, in consequence of its constitution, is impelled to combine things according to their efficient causes. As soon as we observe a certain positive relation among things to one another; as soon as we can represent to ourselves one thing as possible only through the idea we possess of another; we can reduce such a combination to no other idea than that of final causes, or of means and purposes. Although we are not able to perceive and to determine the ground, on which that connection rests, as a thing, independent on our senses; we may still conceive it, in a general manner, as the ground of such a combination as can be represented by us under the idea of connecting final causes; we may thus think of it under the only *symbol*, which can properly denote the basis of this association, namely that of Reason. In this way, however, we have no title to refer the modes and actions we observe in our Reason, to that being (substratum) itself; but we must make use of them only as a symbol, which at least expresses similar relations.

We must, therefore, justly consider the world, as if every thing were arranged in it by the highest Understanding; and we must, with the greatest attention, endeavour to discover in experience those traces, that are every where scattered for the support of this conclusion; in order to prepare our minds for the conviction arising from a very considerable number of individual cases. In this, we shall the better succeed, if, as the ground-work of this inquiry, we exhibit that systematic order, which is already determined by our Reason *a priori*, and in consequence of which determination the moral beings compose the last and absolute purpose, to which all other things ultimately and necessarily refer as the means of the former. But since we can recognize no other moral being than man, we must accordingly regulate our investigations relative to final purposes, and particularly attend to what is connected with *his* nature. Here, however, we must abandon the notion hitherto erroneously maintained by many Theologians, that *every thing* has a necessary relation to man. For, as the world of moral beings certainly consists of more classes than we are acquainted with, we may indeed presuppose, that men are absolute purposes, yet far from being exclusively so; and that nature has not been constituted for the sake of men alone, but that, at the same time, other moral beings have not been disregarded. We may therefore safely admit, that nature has been so formed, that the essential purposes concerning man can be certainly attained, notwithstanding that the accidental purposes must occasionally remain unaccomplished, on account of others that are more important and necessary. For this assertion, which is supported merely upon the principles of our moral nature, and not by any intuitive knowledge of the world itself, experience only furnishes us with arguments which the order of the world displays in individual cases. But the greatest number of phenomena must necessarily remain inexplicable to us, who are acquainted only with the smallest part of the world, and from whom the extensive territory of moral beings is almost wholly concealed; whereas a complete knowledge of their relations to purposes would presuppose not only a thorough knowledge of the world of sense, but likewise that of moral beings. We derive from the contemplation of the world no proofs showing a regular order of moral purposes, but we investigate the cases corresponding with that order, so as to ascertain it in the individual, and to strengthen our knowledge upon what we had already presupposed, in consequence of our moral nature. For, that which affords some knowledge in a general way, gives but a slight degree of conviction; while that, which animates this conviction and renders it applicable to particular cases, i. e. our sensation of it, is produced only by individual instances.

According to these principles, we shall be able to discover traces of divine wisdom in a great number of phenomena, without neglecting on that account our inquiries into nature, which alone can extend our knowledge of things; which previously unfolds the matter of knowledge; and which points out the relations, wherein divine wisdom is evident. The field of physics is immense; and by an appeal to the Deity, who has produced nature itself conformably to final causes, we can set no limits to that field. For, to obtain a complete view of final causes, and to apply them to the explanation of phenomena, is entirely out of our power: we can only mark them as the result arising from our intuitive knowledge of nature, with this limitation; that, when we obtain a

more

more accurate knowledge of the nature of these things, we shall likewise discover a greater variety of final causes, and so on in infinitum.

The contemplation of nature, agreeably to final purposes, is therefore fully established in the constitution of our Reason; although we have no intuition of the being that is the basis of this order. We can conceive this being merely by the idea of Reason in general, as the only possible way of apprehending it; this, however, our knowledge of the nature of that being is not increased; and we only satisfy a subjective, but necessary claim of our Reason; for such an order of things as depends upon a regular succession of final causes, can be thought of by no other relation but that of a causality conformably to ideas; a result, which exactly corresponds with the general idea of an efficient Reason.

CONTENTS.

Introduction.—I. Of the division of philosophy into theoretical and practical.
II. Of the extent of philosophy in general.
III. Of the Critique of the Judging Faculty, being the medium of combining the two parts of philosophy into one system.
IV. Of the Judging Faculty being a legislative power *a priori*.
V. The principle of formal conformation (*Zweckmäßigkeit*) of nature is a transcendental principle of the Judging Faculty.
VI. Of the connection between the sensation of pleasure and the idea of the conformation of nature.
VII. On the aesthetical method of representing this conformation.
VIII. On the logical method of exhibiting the same.
IX. On the connections formed between the legislative acts of the Understanding and Reason, by means of the Judging Faculty.

The following Table exhibits the whole of what relates to the province of
TRANSCENDENTAL PHILOSOPHY

Collective faculties of the Mind.	Faculties of Cognition.	Principles a priori.	Application to
The Faculty of Cognition.	The Understanding.	Legality.	Nature.
The sense of pleasure and displeasure.	The Judging Faculty.	Conformation.	Art.
The faculty of desiring.	Reason.	Final purpose.	Liberty.

DIVISION I. CRITIQUE OF THE AESTHETICAL FACULTY OF JUDGING.

SECT. I. ANALYSIS OF THE AESTHETICAL JUDGING FACULTY.

BOOK I. *Analysis of the Beautiful.*

FIRST MODIFICATION *of the Judgment of Taste according to its* QUALITY.

§ 1. The judgment of taste is *aesthetical*. 2. The approbation determined by this judgment is not influenced by any self-interest relative to the object. 3. The approbation or the satisfaction we express upon what is *agreeable*, is connected with self-interest. 4. The same is the case with regard to what is *good*. 5. Comparison of the three specifically different kinds of satisfaction.

SECOND MODIFICATION *of the Judgment of Taste, namely according to its* QUANTITY.

§ 6. That which is represented as an object of *universal* approbation, independent on collateral notions, is called Beautiful. 7. Comparison of the Beautiful, the Agreeable, and the Good, by the above stated character. 8. The universality of approbation, in a judgment of taste, is represented only in a subjective sense. 9. Investigation of the question: whether in a judgment of taste the sense of pleasure precede the act of judging upon the object, or follow it.

THIRD MODIFICATION *of the Judgments of Taste, according to their* RELATION *to purposes*.

§ 10. Of Conformation in general. 11. The judgment of taste is wholly founded upon the *form* or the *nexus finalis* of an object, (or on the manner of representing that object to the mind). 12. The judgment of taste depends upon principles a priori. 13. 14. This judgment is not related to any emotion of the mind. 15. It is equally unconnected with the idea of perfection. 16. That judgment of taste, by which an object is declared to be beautiful only under a certain condition, cannot be called a pure judgment. 17. On the prototype of Beauty.

FOURTH MODIFICATION *of the Judgment of Taste, according to the* MODALITY *of the satisfaction in the object*.

§ 10. This modality of an aesthetical judgment is not a necessary,

but

but an *exemplary* determination of *all* individuals, respecting a judgment, that is considered as an example of a general rule, the particulars of which cannot be defined. 19. The subjective necessity, which we attribute to an aesthetical judgment, is conditional. 20. The condition of the necessity, which a judgment of taste supposes, is the idea of a common sense. 21. Whether we have grounds, on which we may conclude the reality of a common sense. 22. The necessity of the general approbation, which is conceived in an aesthetical judgment, is a subjective necessity, which, under the supposition of a common sense, is represented as objective.

CORROLLARIES FROM THESE FOUR MODIFICATIONS.

I. *Taste* is the faculty of judging of an object, or of representing it by means of approbation or disapprobation, unconnected with *any self-interest*. The object of such approbation is called *Beautiful*.

II. *Beautiful* is that which affords universal satisfaction, without reducing it to a certain idea.

III. *Beauty* is the conformation or *nexus finalis* of an object, so far as it is observed in it, *without the representation of a purpose*.

IV. *Beautiful* is that which is recognized as an object of *necessary* satisfaction, without combining with it a particular idea.

BOOK II. *Analysis of the Sublime.*

§ 23. Transition from the judging power of the Beautiful to that of the Sublime. 24. Of the division of an inquiry into the sensation of the Sublime. A. *On the mathematical Sublime.* 25. Definition of the Sublime: "*Sublime*, in general, is that which is absolutely great, which admits of no comparison, to think of which only proves a faculty of the mind, which is not subject to any scale of the senses, &c." 26. Of the mathematical computation of natural objects, which is requisite to produce the idea of the Sublime. 27. Of the quality of the satisfaction we receive in judging of the Sublime. B. *On the dynamical Sublime of nature.* 28. Nature, considered as might (*potentia*). 29. On the modality of the judgment respecting the

the Sublime of nature.—*Deduction of the pure aesthetical judgments.*—30. The deduction of aesthetical judgments upon the objects of nature must not be directed to what we call sublime in the latter, but to the Beautiful only. 31. On the proper method of this deduction. 32. *First* peculiarity of an aesthetical judgment: " that it determines its object with respect to the satisfaction found in it, at the same time claiming the approbation of *every body*, as if it were *objective*." 33. *Second* peculiarity; " that it cannot at all be determined by argumental proofs, as if it were merely *subjective*." 34. No objective principle of taste can be discovered. 35. The principle of taste is the subjective principle of the judging faculty in general. 36. How the deduction of aesthetical judgments must be carried on. 37. What is properly asserted a priori, in this judgment, concerning the object. 38. Deduction of aesthetical judgments. 39. How a sensation can be communicated. 40. Of Taste, as a species of *sensus communis*. 41. Of the empirical interest in the Beautiful. 42. Of the intellectual interest. 43. Of art in general. " *Art* is distinguished from *Nature*, like doing (*facere*) from acting or operating in general (*agere*); and the production of the former, i. e. work (*opus*) is distinguished from the latter as operation (*effectus*).—*Art*, as human ingenuity, is further distinguished from *Science*, like the practical from the theoretical part of geometry; for to be acquainted with the principles of navigation, for instance, does not yet form a practical navigator: hence the Sciences imply the knowledge of things, and the Arts teach us the practical application of that knowledge.— Lastly, *Art* is distinguished from *handicraft*; the former may be called *free*, the latter, *mercenary art*." 44. Of the fine arts. 45. By fine arts is understood any art, so far as it, at the same time, is imitative of nature. 46, 47. The fine arts are the efforts of genius. 48. Of the distinction subsisting between genius and taste. " To *judge* of beautiful objects, as such, requires *taste*; but the art of *producing* such objects, supposes *genius*." 49. Of the faculties of the mind, which compose what is called genius. 50. Taste and genius must be combined in the productions of the fine arts. 51. Of the division of fine the arts:

" 1.) the arts of language, viz. *Oratory* and *Poetry*; 2.) the arts of sensible imitation, which are either those of *true* or *illusory* exhibitions, the former are called *Plastic*, the latter *Painting*:—*Plastic* includes *Statuary* and *Architecture*; painting consists either in copying beauteous nature, or in beautifully arranging her productions; i. e. in the respective arts of *Painting* or *Pleasure-gardening*;—3.) the beautiful combination of external sensations, viz. the arts of *Music* and *Dying*."
52. Of the combination of the fine arts in one and the same production. 53. Comparison of the fine arts with one another, with regard to their aesthetical value.

SECT. II. DIALECTIC OF THE AESTHETICAL JUDGING FACULTY.

§ 55—57. Representation and Solution of the Antinomy of Taste. 58. On the Idealism of conformation in nature as well as art, being the only principle of the aesthetical faculty of judging. 59. Of Beauty as the symbol of Morality. 60. *Append.* Of the methodical doctrine of Taste.

DIVISION II. CRITIQUE OF THE TELEOLOGICAL FACULTY OF JUDGING.

§ 61. Of the objective conformation of nature.

Sect. I. Analysis of the teleological faculty of Judging.

§ 62. Of the objective conformation, which is merely formal, in distinction from what is material. 63. Of the relative conformation of nature, in distinction from the internal. 64. Of the peculiar character of things, as purposes of nature. 65. Things, as natural purposes, are organized beings. 66. Of the principle of judging of the internal conformation of organized beings. 67. Of the teolological principle of judging of Nature in general, as a system of purposes. 68. Of the principle of Teleology, as an internal principle of Natural Philosophy.

Sect. II. Dialectic of the teleological Faculty of Judging.

§ 69. The antinomy of the Judging Faculty. 70, 71. Representation and solution of this antinomy. 72. Of the various
systems

systems respecting the conformation of nature. 73. None of these systems is satisfactory. 74. The cause of the impossibility of treating this idea, "that nature is *technically* arranged," in a dogmatical manner, lies in our incapacity of explaining the design or aim of nature. 75. The idea of an objective conformation of nature is a critical principle of Reason, belonging to the reflex Faculty of Judging. 76. Illustrating remarks. 77. Of the peculiarity of the human understanding, from which the idea of the purposes of nature arises. 78. On the principle of the universal mechanism of matter, united with the teleological principle in the technical (architectonic) arrangement of nature.

APPENDIX. *Methodical doctrine of the teleological Faculty of Judging.*

§ 79. Whether Teleology ought to be treated as a branch of Physics. 80. Of the necessity of classing the principle of mechanism under that of teleology, when we attempt to explain a thing as a design of nature. 81. On the association of mechanism with the teleological principle, accounting for natural purposes, as being the productions of nature. 82. Of the teleological system in the external relations of organized beings. 83. Of the last purpose (design) of nature as a teleological system. 84. Of the final purposes of the existence of a world, i. e. of the creation itself. 85. Of physico-theology. 86. Of ethico-theology. 87. Of the moral proof of the existence of God. 88. The validity of this moral proof is limited. 89. Of the use of the moral argument. 90. Of the manner of admitting things as true, in a moral proof of the existence of God. 91. Of the manner of considering things as true, by means of a practical belief.

XXVI. *Ueber eine Entdeckung, nach der alle Critik der reinen Vernunft durch eine ältere entbehrlich gemacht werden soll.* On a certain discovery, by means of which every (new) Critique of pure Reason is said to be rendered unnecessary by an earlier one. 8vo. *Koenigsberg.* 1790.

We merely take notice of this publication, here, for the sake of completeness. It can scarcely be considered as forming a distinct part of Kant's systematic works; it is neither mentioned as such by the numerous German commentators upon the Critical Philosophy, nor has Mr Nitsch of London availed himself of this (apparently polemic) production, in his late view of the Kantian principles.—For this reason, we do not hesitate to pass it over in silence, and to devote a considerable degree of attention to the following work, on Religion, which is of infinitely greater importance.

XXVII. (10.) *Die Religion innerhalb den Grenzen der blossen Vernunft.* Religion considered within the bounds of mere Reason. *Koenigsberg.* 1793. 2d Edit. enlarged. 1794, pp. 314, and xxvi pp. Preface.

It cannot be a matter of indifference to a philosopher, to know what relation the prevailing religion of the age bears to the speculative notions of Reason, that are propagated in the philosophic systems of his cotemporaries. Although the inquiries of this nature be conducted independently of any positive religious creed, we may yet congratulate ourselves upon the discovery, when that positive religion, which guides a very considerable part of mankind, and which has produced so many excellent moral effects, is not found to be altogether inconsistent with the principles, maintained by the most profound and eminent philosophers. We may at the same time learn, to give a more practical explanation upon those symbolical points, that have hitherto met with no useful application, and that have occasioned many fruitless and bloody contests.

No man of candour and impartiality will censure the design of a writer, who employs his philosophic maxims (if they be otherwise well established upon a critical basis), in order to serve as principles, for explaining ambiguous doctrines and positive institutions. For, if the Deity has immediately intrusted man with so valuable a gift as religion actually is, it must have been corrupted by men themselves, who have delivered it to their posterity, with such additions as are inconsistent with the principles of Reason; and the true original sense of such traditions can be discovered only

through

through the proper exercise of Reason. Every attempt, therefore, of restoring harmony between the positive tenets of Religion and those of philosophy, must be considered as highly beneficial to mankind; because, in this manner only, the design of that revelation can be consistently attained.

Our satisfaction, too, must be the more complete, when we have an opportunity of observing, that such a revelation has not only been preserved in its purity during the course of many centuries, but likewise has been the means of exercising the rational faculties of man, upon the most profound subjects of inquiry.—If we compare the principal tenets of the Christian Religion with the principles of the Kantian system, we shall be agreeably surprised to find, that the former are perfectly consistent with the latter, and that this author satisfies all the claims, which can be made on philosophy, to establish a pure religious doctrine. For the result of KANT's investigations, upon this head, is nearly the following:

1st, That Christianity is throughout a *moral Religion*, such as Reason requires of every religious establishment whatever. It is, among the numerous religions in the world, the only one, which derives its principles from pure morals, and which represents to man his destination as attainable only by moral means. It indeed presupposes, that he has the power and ability of doing, what the law of philanthropy commands him; though, at the same time, Religion apprizes him of that resistance, which natural inclinations or *carnal* desires oppose to the exercise of Reason. It further appropriates to him, in express terms, the capacity of overcoming these difficulties; and as the human understanding can arrive at no objective knowledge of such a power, Scripture lays the foundation of it in something beyond the reach of the senses, while it gives man the assurance, that the Deity may also endow him with faculties, which materially differ from those of mere sensitive beings; in order to accomplish, by the power of his will, whatever he judges to be morally right and and salutary. In this manner alone, Reason can form a complete and clear notion, that the moral power is a *supersensible* agent, whose origin or, in the language of KANT, whose possibility we cannot by any means conceive.

2d. The true destination of man is, conformably to the principles of Christianity, not sought for in the sensible, but in the super-sensible part of nature. Man must acquire happiness by his moral conduct, but he ought not to expect the former in this world; not to derive his hopes of it from his sensitive, but from his moral nature. For, according to the Christian doctrine, his sole business here consists in preparing and making himself worthy of it, through a purely moral life.

3d. The Christian Religion throughout presupposes a moral government of the world, and the idea of the moral order of things serves as its basis: this order, however, can be realized or accomplished only in relation to the whole existence of rational beings. Exactly in the same manner is this proposition determined by our Reason.

4th. The Religion of Christ enjoins us to consider good will to all mankind as the supreme principle of all our actions. It enjoins us to unite self-love, in equal proportion with universal benevolence, or rather to make the former subservient to the purposes of the latter: and this is precisely the dictate of Reason, and what Kant asserts to be the first moral precept. Through this practical law alone, the Christians determine the attributes of the Deity, since they represent him as the moral creator, preserver, and ruler of the world.

5th. Thus, in the religion of Christ, morality is laid down as the cognoscible ground, on which we establish our knowledge of the Deity. We can boast, indeed, of no perceptive cognition of that Being; yet we are not contented with a mere speculative notion of him, whose attributes we can clearly exhibit in the idea of a moral intelligent power. Lastly,

6th. The whole aim of the Christian Religion is the moral improvement and perfection of man. The whole purpose of Religion, when contemplated by Reason, can be no other than to render man morally better, or to improve his moral worth. It must admit of being employed as the means of strengthening his moral faculties, of removing the obstacles that frequently occur in the practice of morality, and of fortifying the powers of Reason.

Even

Even the dogmatical part of the Christian doctrine is of such a nature as to display, in the greater number of instances, a relative application to morals; and the principal tenets of it, have a manifest tendency to solve moral difficulties. These appear at so early a period among men, that attempts to account for them very soon follow. Such explanations, in general, are extremely ludicrous, especially in the infancy of Reason, when fancy supplies its place, and before experience has been made our guide. Imagination scarcely listens to the suggestions of Reason; and, in this situation, men are easily pleased with any plausible answer, which their ancestors have contrived from the rich stores of mythology. Though their knowledge of objects is not thereby increased, yet the hypotheses thus contrived are usually ingenious, so that they might afford some satisfaction, if they were founded upon any thing but fancy.

This infant age of reasoning, if it may be called so, is attended with the advantage, that it does not conceal the difficulties, for which it cannot account. Reason, being gradually enlightened by philosophy, is conscious of this chimerical method of explaining things; but as it imagines any other explanation to be impossible; it rather considers the difficulty itself as fictitious, in order to show, that all attempts at explaining it must be dispensed with.

By gradual advances, Reason discovers that such difficulties really exist, and that all sophistical disputes upon them are of no avail. At the same time, we find that the former are of such a nature, as to admit of no other solution than that by practical ideas, and that these ideas are expressed in those fanciful explanations of mythology, by the representation of *sensible* objects.

Now, since every thing connected with morals, as well as every conclusion drawn from that source, is justly denominated by the epithet ' divine;' it is easy to perceive, how those mythological objects, together with the fictitious productions of fancy, could be called divine revelations. For there really is a moral text or meaning at the foundation of them, but which can be disclosed only in a more improved state of Reason.

From this deduction, it becomes perfectly evident, in what manner we meet with two very different explanations of such books, as
contain

contain the like solutions of moral propositions, under the title of Revelation. One of these explanations namely boasts of stating the literal sense of the Writ, and is styled the *grammatical* interpretation: the other traces the ideas, that may originally have occasioned those fictions, and considers the subjects of mythology as the symbols of those ideas. And this is justly called the *moral* interpretation. If now each of the two pursues its own method of inquiry, disputes may easily arise among the different interpreters; for they will frequently find opposite meanings in one and the same passage.

These dissensions in the interpretation of Scripture, daily display their baneful effects, however easily they might be settled, if the interpreters were not averse to enter into a proper agreement upon certain points. For, no man will deny, that all Revelation rests upon the inward state of our mind; that all positive Religions are more or less perfect expressions of Revelation; and that, therefore, the true interpretation of it can be discovered only by our own subjective operations. Hence it is, that those only, who are well acquainted with the nature of the human mind, can find the true sense of Revelations. Reason is here likewise the supreme tribunal, from which no further appeal can be made. The doctrines of the original evil, of reconciliation, and many other principles, peculiar to the Christian Religion, are founded on a basis, that admits of very excellent and useful reflections, upon the moral constitution of man, and upon the manner in which his destination has been provided for. Nay, from these doctrines, it is evident, how those opinions, which appear to have a common origin in human nature, have ever been represented through certain narratives and allegories; and how the minds of men in all ages resorted to them, as if they had been conducted by an invisible hand, without being uniformly conscious of their true meaning. And is there any greater service, which the philosophic inquirer can render mankind, than to investigate these traces of Reason, which, by their sacred antiquity, have so important an influence on human affairs; though their origin be, for the most part, involved in obscurity. From this investigation, the only explanation must result, which can contribute to the attainment of that ultimate end, for which man is originally

ginally defigned. If, in this way of explaining symbols, we fearch merely for figns of fuch truths, as are previoufly difcovered by our mind, the errors or miftakes cannot be fo detrimental, as if we aimed at finding the truth itfelf, by means of thefe symbols. For, in the former cafe, imagination can merely miflead us to denote a true thing by a falfe symbol; whereas, in the latter cafe, we are expofed to the danger of confounding a fymbol (to which our fancy is but too fondly attached) with the truth itfelf, and thus of falling into mere chimerical notions. Let us therefore fearch in the regions of truth; and, directing our views to the monuments of antiquity, inquire, whether among them we can difcover no figns correfponding with our moral attainments. Thus we may facilitate the accefs to the fanctuary of truth, in as much as our new method of explaining will afcertain, whether we have fucceeded in exploring the juft character of religious truths, and whether the true fenfe of the refpective fymbols has ever been clearly underftood.

CONTENTS.

SECT. I. ON THE CONJUNCTION OR LEAGUE BETWEEN THE BAD AND GOOD PRINCIPLE; OR ON THE RADICAL EVIL IN HUMAN NATURE.

1. Of the original difpofition (inclination) towards the good in human nature.
2. Of the propenfity to vice.
3. Whether man is *naturally* vicious.
4. Of the origin of evil in human nature.

General Remarks. On the manner of reftoring to its vigour the *original* difpofition towards the good.

SECT. II. ON THE CONTEST BETWEEN THE GOOD PRINCIPLE AND THE BAD, FOR THE DOMINION OVER MANKIND.

1. Of the legal claim of the good principle to the dominion over mankind.
2. Of the legal claim of the bad principle to that dominion, and the conteft between the two principles.

SECT. III. ON THE VICTORY OF THE GOOD PRINCIPLE OVER THE BAD, AND THE FOUNDATION OF A KINGDOM OF GOD UPON EARTH.

Chap. I. Philosophical exhibition of the victory of the good principle, by the foundation of a kingdom of God upon Earth.

1. Of the ethical state of nature.
2. Man must leave the ethical state of nature, in order to become a member of an ethical *commonwealth*.
3. The idea of an ethical commonwealth is that of a *people of God*, under ethical laws.
4. The idea of a people of God is (through human regulations) no otherwise to be exhibited in practice, but by the formation of a Church.
5. The constitution of every church uniformly begins with some or other historical belief (revelation) which may be called the church-belief, and this is most suitably founded on a Holy Writ.
6. The pure religious belief is the supreme interpreter of church-belief.
7. The gradual transition of church-belief, to the exclusive prevalence of the pure religious belief, indicates the approach of a kingdom of God.

Chap. II. Historical exhibition of the gradual foundation of the predominance of the good principle upon Earth.

SECT IV. OF THE WORSHIP AND SPURIOUS WORSHIP UNDER THE DOMINION OF THE GOOD PRINCIPLE, OR OF RELIGION AND PRIESTHOOD*.

A. *Of the divine service in Religion in general.*
  1. The Christian Religion considered as a Natural Religion.
  2. The Christian Religion considered as a Learned Religion.

B. *Of the spurious worship of God, in a statutory Religion established by men.*
  § 1. Of the general subjective ground of *religious fancy*.

2.

---

* *Pfaffenthum*, in German, is not literally 'priesthood,' nor does it signify 'priestcraft;' but it expresses the usurped dominion of the clergy, by which they pretend to be in the exclusive possession of the means of dispensing absolution from sins and divine grace.

2. The moral principles of Religion, confidered in oppofition to religious fancy.

3. Of *Priefthood*, as being an order of men engaged in the *fpurious* worfhip of the *good* principle.

4. Of the guide afforded by confcience, in matters of belief.

XXVIII. *Zum ewigen Frieden*, &c. Project for a perpetual peace. A philofophical Effay. 104 pp. 8vo. *Königsberg*, 1795.

Of this original work, which is fo much and juftly admired on the continent, we already poffefs an Englifh tranflation. And if the appearance of this production in foreign verfions could eftablifh any proof of its merits, I might add, that " Kant's project for a perpetual peace" has been likewife tranflated into French, and indeed with the fanction of the author, who has furnifhed the French tranflator with a *new* Supplement, which contains, " *a fecret article for a perpetual peace.*"

Many of our political readers muft remember, that the idea of a perpetual peace has formerly employed the pen of the GOOD ABBOT DE ST. PIERRE; and that, at a ftill earlier period, the moft patriotic King of whom France can boaft, HENRY IV, was ferioufly engaged in modelling this beneficent plan, which he propofed to fubmit to the confideration of his cotemporary potentates, if an untimely death had not fruftrated that philanthropic defign.— Though our fage politicians have always confidered plans of this kind as the fanciful productions of good-natured fanatics, it may on the other hand be obferved, that by difputing on the poffibility of a perpetual peace, the neceffity of a perpetual warfare muft be admitted as a maxim; becaufe, without being continually prepared for war, the different ftates of Europe could not long exift together. This maxim, however, is as abominable in theory, as it is practically deftructive of every principle of morality. For, if *all* independent ftates adopt or continue to practice fuch a maxim, and if their views be conftantly directed to the execution of it, their political exiftence itfelf muft be extremely precarious. From this fource, I am inclined to derive the frequent revolutions in the political world, the frequent returns from a state of intellectual and moral improvement to their former barbarism, and the perpetual animosities (emphatically called, *natural* enmities) between man and man, which are so industriously transmitted from one generation to another; especially in the frontier-provinces of different nations.—Man is a fighting animal! is the general outcry of all those who are interested, whether directly or indirectly, in propagating this absurd and pernicious doctrine. Even admitting, that man is naturally prone to exercise his physical powers; that he has this propensity in common with the lower animals; that he occasionally manifests the desire of revenge and conquest, not unlike the rapacious tyger or the victorious lion; and that he cannot easily overcome these natural inclinations, as long as his inhuman feats are more admired and encouraged than the dignified, though less alluring, exertions of his intellect;—does it follow from these *primitive* dispositions of savage man, that perpetual warfare is a necessary evil in the *present* state of society? I hope for the honour of humanity, that none but the callous financiers of deluded nations, or the avaricious contractors of armies and navies, with their numerous train of connections, will be hardy enough to draw so false a conclusion.

When we consider those, who direct the affairs of nations, in a moral as well as legislative capacity, it is rather surprising, that the important plan of a perpetual peace has never been duly weighed: while many subjects of less consequence, and comparatively trifling matters, daily occupy their attention. Nobody will deny, that the ideas of right and wrong, of just and unjust, are equally applicable to a plurality of states, as to different individuals of one or several countries. The only obstacle to the *just* application of these ideas must, therefore, lie in the diversity of opinions, arising among those *corrupted* servants of the state, to whom the management of external affairs is intrusted. Why, therefore, do the rulers of nations not agree upon a general federation of states? —Why do they not, like every other *reasonable* being, submit to arbitration, by choosing the arbiters from the bosom of disinterested states; in order to settle such differences as their own ministers cannot determine? This would be the only rational and proper method;

method; a method, which is daily practised in private life, by those very men, who seem to oppose its introduction in diplomatic transactions. Nay, if the arm of violence and rapacity were permitted to decide the quarrels of individuals, all civil institutions and social compacts would soon be dissolved. And does not the same reasoning apply to every government, whether monarchical, aristrocratic, or democratic?—have we not sufficient testimonies upon historical record, that dissolution and annihilation have hitherto been their ultimate fate?

Induced by such considerations, the venerable Kant, after having observed the political changes of Europe, for upwards of half a century, steps forward with a plan drawn up in a diplomatic form. His noble design of stopping the prodigal effusion of human blood, and his aim at convincing the governors of nations, that the practicability of this plan merely depends upon the exertions of their moral will, are equally conspicuous. The great modern improvements in Ethics throughout society, particularly in the higher ranks; the view of the innumerable sufferings and exterminations accompanying the present state of warfare in Europe; and finally the conviction, that his "Project" is truly practicable and morally unexceptionable; these were sufficient motives to rouse the "hoary philosopher of the North," and to animate him with new vigour for this grand and benevolent attempt.

The author exhibits the *Preliminary* and *Definitive Articles* for a perpetual peace, in two Sections, which he accompanies with proper illustrations. The preliminary articles are as follows:

1. "No treaty of peace shall be considered as valid, that has been concluded with a secret reserve of matters for a future war.
2. "No independent state shall ever be permitted to be transferred to the dominion of another state, whether by inheritance, exchange, purchase, or donation.
3. "Standing armies (miles perpetuus) shall in time be entirely discharged.
4. "No national or state-debts shall be contracted, that relate to the external or foreign affairs of the state.
5. "No state shall, by force of arms, interfere with either the constitution or government of other states.

6. "No state, at war with another, shall make use of such hostilities, as must destroy their reciprocal confidence in a future peace; for instance, the employing of assassins, poisoners, the violation of cartels, the instigation of treasonable practices, rebellion in the inimical state, &c."

The conclusion of a *definitive peace* presupposes it as a postulate: "that all men, who are able to produce reciprocal effects upon each other, must necessarily be subject to some civil institutions." All civil institutions, however, as far as regards the *persons* submitting to them, may be reduced to three classes: 1.) those concerning the right of the citizen in the state; 2.) those relative to the right of nations; and 3.) those ascertaining the rights of the citizen of the world (cosmopolite). Conformably to this introduction, the author proposes *three Definitive Articles*.

I. *The civil constitution of every state ought to be republican.*—By a republican constitution is here understood such a one, as is founded upon the principles of *liberty, dependence*, and *equality*. By means of that *liberty*, acquired by the constitutional law, all the members of a state must be entitled to the privilege of obeying no other external or bye-laws than those, to which they have given their consent. By virtue of their legal *dependence*, all members of a society are subject to only one common legislation. And by their legal *equality*, among men as citizens of the state, there must subsist such a relation, that none of them can lawfully oblige the other, without subjecting himself to the law, by which the other party *may* reciprocally compel him in a similar instance. This, therefore, is the only constitution, which forms the basis of every other in civil society; and it is also the only one, that can lead to a perpetual peace. For, in a government, where the consent of the citizens of the state is required for declaring war, they will be very cautious in giving their approbation to those horrid measures, in consequence of which they themselves must bear all the calamities of a bloody contest.

In order to prevent any misconstruction of terms, KANT distinguishes a *republican* from a *democratic* constitution, by discriminating between the *forms of government* (*imperii*), and those

of

of *administration* (*regiminis*); the former of which are determined by the distinction of *persons*, who hold the supreme power of the state, but the latter, by the *mode of governing* the people by a supreme head, whoever this may be. The forms of government, or those of the former kind, are, *autocrasy* or the power of the prince, *aristocracy* or the power of the nobles, and *democracy* or the power of the people: those of the latter kind, namely the forms of administration, are *republicanism* and *despotism*. The former of these again consists, according to the essential characters above described, in the separation of the executive power from the legislative; the latter, namely despotism, is the arbitrary execution of the laws, which the sovereign himself has enacted; so that his private will becomes the public law of the nation.—Concerning *democracy* then, Kant affirms, that it *necessarily* leads to *despotism*; because it establishes a legislative and executive power, by which all have a share in forming resolutions relative to *one*, and even against this one, who consequently would not agree with them, so that *all* are said to partake of the legislation, when in fact they do not so; which is in contradiction to the general will itself and to liberty.

II. *The rights of nations ought to be founded upon a federation of independent states.*—The author's ideas in this article are expressed with equal boldness, energy, and truth. The result of them is this: In the relative condition of states to one another, there can be rationally no other method of extricating themselves from the lawless condition, that engenders continual wars, than to imitate individual man in the resignation of his wild (unconstrained) liberty; to accomodate themselves to public compulsory laws; and thus to form a *state of nations*, gradually increasing, and at length comprehending all the nations of the earth. Since, however, according to their notions of the right of nations, they are averse to submit like individuals to the laws of compulsion; and since they reject *in hypothesi* what is just *in thesi*; let them at least adopt the *negative* substitute of a federation (congress) for the prevention of war, instead of the *positive* establishment of an *universal republic*. Such a congress may at least save us from total ruin, by checking that hostile

tile difposition of man, which fhuns the operation of the law; it may gradually fpread its beneficent influence to diftant nations; though it will neverthelefs be in conftant danger of being interrupted, by the capricious oppofition of a lawlefs monarch.

III. *The cofmopolitical right fhall be limited to conditions of univerfal hofpitality.*—The cofmopolitical right is that of a ftranger, by which he is intitled to a friendly reception at his arrival upon foreign ground. It is not ftrictly the right of hofpitality, but that of vifiting one another, which belongs to all men, in offering their company, by virtue of their common inhabitation of the furface of the earth. The *inhofpitality* of fea-coafts, for inftance that of Barbary, and the *inhofpitable* conduct of cultivated and chiefly of commercial nations of our quarter of the globe, who change their *vifits* into *conquefts*, is confequently againft the law of nature. As, however, the means of communication among the nations of the earth are fo much improved, that the violation of a right on *one* fpot of the globe is now felt in *all* countries; it hence follows, that the idea of a cofmopolitical law is not a whimfical or extravagant reprefentation of a right, but a necefsary fupplement to a code, that remains to be written, and that relates to the rights of ftates and nations, as well as to the rights of man in general. Under this condition only, we may flatter ourfelves with the hopes of a continual, though gradual, approximation to a perpetual peace.

In the further illuftrations annexed to thefe articles, the author maintains, that both morals and politics, fo far from being in oppofition to this plan, rather tend to confirm and to render it univerfal; " for, 'fays he,' the guarantee of this compact is the grand and ingenious artift, nature herfelf, who by her mechanical courfe evidently manifefts her purpofed aim of reftoring harmony among men, even againft their will, and in the very bofom of their contentions. The provifional difpofitions made by nature for this purpofe, are the following: 1) that fhe has provided for the fubfiftence of man in all climates; 2) that fhe has difperfed them, through wars, in every direction, even to the moft inhofpitable countries, in order to people them; and 3) that fhe has thus compelled them to enter into reciprocal

ciprocal engagements, which are more or less established by law."

The many valuable hints and philosophical reflections, contained in this little work, it is impossible to abridge. And as we possess an English translation of it, I must refer the curious reader to the book itself; at the same time assuring him, that he will find the arts of courts and the juggles of statesmen exposed, in a manner altogether original.

XXIX. (11.) *Metaphysische Anfangsgründe der Rechtslehre.* Metaphysical Elements of Jurisprudence. 8vo. *Königsberg,* 1797. xii pp. Preface; LII. pp. Introduction; and 235 pp. Text.

This work affords another proof of the very extensive application, of which the Kantian philosophy is susceptible. Having in his former publications established, on a critical basis (that of a pure and practical Reason), the principles of Physics, of Taste, of Morality, and of rational Religion, the author proceeds in the present, to deduce from the same source the elements of Jurisprudence; and not only lays down the private rights of individuals, but unfolds also the principles, which ought to determine the internal arrangements of Civil Society, and regulate the intercourse of nations.

The mode, in which Prof. KANT treats the subject, will appear from the following observation: "A System of Jurisprudence, the first part of the Science of Morals, derived from Reason, and which might be termed the Metaphysics of Law, is still a desideratum in philosophy. But as the idea of law, though pure, has a relation to practice; i. e. is applicable to the cases occurring in experience, a metaphysical system of it, in its division, must also have a reference to the empirical variety of those cases, in order to make the division complete, which is an indispensable requisite in the formation of a System of Reason. Completeness of division, however, in what is empirical, is impossible; and where it is attempted, or at least an approximation to it, such ideas cannot be considered as integral parts in a System, but merely as examples.

The only proper appellation, therefore, for the first part of the Metaphysics of Morals, is '*Metaphysical Elements of Jurisprudence*;' because, with respect to the application to these cases, there can only be an approximation to a System, not a System itself."

Having, in a general introduction developed the principles of the Moral Science, and having shown the necessity of a Metaphysical System of Morals, i. e, of a practical philosophy derived from ideas *a priori* merely, and which has not nature, but the freedom of the human will, for its object; the author makes the following distinction between Justice and the other virtues, between Ethics and Jurisprudence.—" All legislation, however it may agree with respect to the actions, being in every case external, may yet be distinguished with regard to the motives. That legislation, which constitutes an action a duty, and at the same time makes this duty the motive, is *Ethical*. But that, which does not include in the rule the idea of duty, which on the contrary admits another motive than this idea, is *Juridical*. With respect to the latter, it is easy to perceive, that this motive, different from the idea of duty, must be derived from the pathological grounds, by which the will is determined, viz. inclination and disinclination, and among these from those of the latter kind; because it is a legislation which is compulsory, and does not influence the conduct by the allurements of reward.—The mere conformity of an action to the rule, without regard to the motive, is called its *legality*; but that, in which the idea of duty, arising from the rule, is at the same time the motive of the action, is its *morality*. The duties, according to a Juridical legislation, can only be external, because this legislation does not require, that the idea of duty, which is internal, should be in itself the principle, by which the will of the agent is determined; and as a proper motive for the rule is nevertheless necessary, it can only be externally connected with that rule. Ethical legislation, on the other hand, makes our internal actions also duties, not as it were excluding the external, but proceeding on what is duty in general. And as Ethical legislation includes in its rule the internal motive of action, the idea of duty, which determination can by no means be introduced into an external legislation; so this Ethical legislation cannot be external, not even that of a Divine will; although indeed it assumes for motives, *as being duties*, those duties which depend upon another, namely an external legislation. It is not a duty of virtue to keep one's promise, but an obligation of justice, of law, to the performance of which one may be compelled. Yet to do this, where no compulsion is to be apprehended, is a virtuous action, a proof of virtue. Jurisprudence and Ethics then are distinguished, not so much by the different duties they enjoin, as by the difference of the legislation, which connects with the rule the one or the other motive."

Next follows a particular '*Introduction to Jurisprudence*,' in which the following subjects are discussed.

SECT. I. § A. Of *Jurisprudence*. B. Of *Justice*.—The idea of what is just or right, so far as it refers to a corresponding obligation, includes first, the merely external and practical relation of one person to another, in so far as their actions, as facts, can have mediately or immediately an influence on each other. But secondly, it does not imply the relation of the will of one individual to the *wish* or mere *want* of another, as in the actions of charity or insensibility, but merely to the *will* of that other. Thirdly, in this reciprocal relation of wills, the *matter* of the will, i. e. the end, which every body has in view with the object, which he wills, does not come under consideration. For instance, the question is not, whether one gains or loses by the commodities, which he purchased from me for the exercise of his trade, but merely according to the *form* in the relation of each will, so far only as it is considered as free, whether the action of the one be consistent with the freedom of the other, according to a general law.—C. *General principles of Justice*.—Every action is just or right, according to the maxim of which the freedom of will of one individual is compatible with the freedom of another, agreeably to a general law. B. *Justice or law*, necessarily presupposes compulsion or force.—E. *Strict* justice or law, may also be represented as the possibility of a reciprocally exerted force, consistent with the freedom of every man, and with general rules or laws.

SECT. II. 1. *Of Equity*. 2. *Of the law of necessity*.
SECT. III. DIVISION OF JURISPRUDENCE.—A. *General division of the duties of justice*. B. *General division of laws and rights*. 1.) Law, as

a systematic doctrine is divided into the Law of Nature, which depends entirely on principles *a priori*, and positive or statutary law, which proceeds from the will of a legislator. 2.) Of rights, as the moral power of laying others under an obligation, the chief division is into the *original* and *acquired*; the former of which every man inherits by nature, independent of any legal act; the latter cannot be attained without such an act.—The only original right, that is born with man, is freedom or independence on any other arbitrary will, so far as it is consistent with the liberty of every individual, according to a general law.

Further Contents of the work.

PART I. OF THE PRIVATE RIGHT OF PROPERTY IN GENERAL.

CHAP. I. *Of the mode of possessing something external as property.*

§ 1. My property is that, with which I am so connected, that the use, which another might make of it against my will, would injure me. The subjective condition of the possibility of use, in general, is *possession*. §. 2,—3. Juridical postulate of practical reason. It is possible to have every external object of my will as my property; i. e. the maxim is contrary to justice, according to which, if it were a law, an external object of the will behoved to be in itself without an owner (res nullius). § 4. Exposition of the idea of external property. Of the external objects of my will there can be only three: 1.) a corporeal thing without me; 2.) the will of another to a determined act (praestatio); 3. the situation of another in relation to me, according to the Categories of Substance, Causality, and Community between me and external objects, agreeable to the laws of freedom. § 5. Definition of the idea of external property. External property is that without me, to hinder me from using which, as I chuse, would be unjust, or an injury. § 6. Deduction of the idea of the mere legal or civil possession of an external object. § 7. Application of the principle of the possibility of external property to the objects of experience. § 8. To have something external as property, is only possible in a juridical state, under a public legislative power, i. e. in civil society. § 9. In the state of nature, nothing but a merely *provisional* though real external, property can take place.

CHAP.

CHAP. II. *Of the mode of acquiring external property.*

§ 10. General principles of external acquisition.—I acquire something originally, when I cause that to become mine, which formerly was the property of no other person.—Division of the acquisition of external property: 1.) according to the *matter* (the object) I acquire either a corporeal thing (substance), or the performance of another person (causality), or this other person, i. e. his or her state, so far as I obtain a right to rule over that person; 2.) according to the *form* or mode of acquisition, I have either a *real* right, or a *personal* right, or *both* real and personal right to the possession, not the use, of another person or thing.

Sect. I. *Of real rights.* § 11. A real right is the right to the private use of a thing, in the common possession of which (whether original or acquired) I am with all others. § 12. The first acquisition of a thing can be no other than that of the soil. § 13. Every part of the soil may be originally acquired, and the ground of the possibility of this acquisition is, that the soil in general was originally common. § 14. The legal act of this acquisition is *occupancy*. § 15. It is in civil society alone, that any *peremptory* acquisition can be made: in a state of nature it can only be *provisional*. § 16. Explanation of the idea of an original acquisition of the soil. § 17. Deduction of this idea.

Sect. II. *Of personal rights.* § 18. A personal right is the possession of the will of another, as the power of determining that will through mine to a certain action, according to the laws of freedom. —Of the transference of will by contract. § 19. Of the constituents of a contract. § 20. Of the causality of the will of another, which is acquired. § 21. In a contract, a thing is not acquired by the acceptance of the promise, but by the delivery of what has been promised.

Sect. III. *Of real—personal right.* § 22. This right is that of the possession of an external object as a *thing*, and of the use of it as a person. § 23. Of the right of the Family-Society. § 24,—27. Title *first*: of the right of marriage. § 28—29. Title *second*: of the rights of parentage. § 30. Title *third*: of the rights of a Master of a Family. § 31, 32. Dogmatical division of all the rights

acquirable

acquirable by contracts. I. Of Money. II. Of literary property.

Sect. IV. Of the ideal acquisition of an external object of the will. I. § 33. Of prescription, or the mode of acquiring property by length of possession. II. § 34. Of acquisition by Inheritance. III. § 35, 36. Of posthumous reputation.

CHAP. III. *Of the subjectively conditioned acquisition, by the sentence of a Public Court of Justice.*

A. § 37. Of the contract of Donation. B. § 38. Of the contract of Loan (commodatum). C. § 39. Of the re-acquisition or reclaiming of property lost (vindicatio). D. § 40. Of the acquisition of security by oath (cautio juratoria). § 41, 42. Transition from property in a state of nature, to that in a juridical state, or civil society in general.

PART II. OF PUBLIC LAW.

Sect. I. § 43, 44. *Of the Constitutional Law of a State.* § 45—47. Of a State as a collection of men.—Of the powers in a State, Legislative, Executive, and Judicial. " The only rational plan of government is that, in which the combined will of the people determines the law." § 48, 49. Of co-ordinate and subordinate powers.—*General Remarks.*—A. Of the supreme power; of the social compact, and the duty of obedience. Of redress of grievances. Of sedition and rebellion.—According to the principles established by KANT, " A change in the Constitution of a State, " which its faults may sometimes render necessary, can only in " justice be accomplished by the Sovereign, by means of *reform*; " not by the people, by means of a *revolution*; and if it take place, " it can only affect the executive, not the legislative power. At " the same time, if a revolution has once been brought about, and " a new constitution established, the injustice of this revolution in " its beginning and accomplishment, does not free the subjects " from the obligation to accommodate themselves, as good citi- " zens, to the new order of things." B. Of the rights of the sovereign power to the territory of the State. Of the rights of taxation. Of Finance and Police. C. Of the maintenance of the poor; of Foundling Hospitals; of a religious establishment. D. Of the

the diftribution of offices; of rank in the State; of Nobility. E. Of criminal law, and a penal code; of the right of punifhing and pardoning. § 50. Of the relation of a citizen to his native and other countries, in point of right and obligation. § 51. Of the different forms of government. § 52. Of the attainment of that rational form, which the fpirit of an original compact requires, which makes *freedom* alone the principle, i. e. the bafis, and condition of all *force*.—Of the reprefentative Syftem.

Sect. II. *Of the law of Nations, or international law.* § 53, 54. Nations, in their external relation to each other, are in a ftate of nature, not unlike lawlefs favages, among whom the right of the ftrongeft is eftablifhed; confequently, a confederacy of ftates becomes neceffary, in order to protect one another againft external attacks, conformably to the idea of an original focial compact. § 55—58. Of the right of making war, both with regard to the fubjects of a State, and foreign nations. § 59, 60. Of the right of peace. § 61. Of the injuftice of a ftate of warfare. "*There fhall be no war*, is the irrefiftible *veto* of morally-practical Reafon."—Of the mode of bringing nations, like individuals, from a ftate of nature to a *juridical* ftate.—Of the eftablifhment and maintenance of a perpetual peace, by means of a permanent Congrefs of States.

Sect. III. *Of Cofmopolitical law, or the rights of the citizen of the world.* § 62. Of the right of mutual intercourfe and commerce, as belonging to all mankind.

Conclufion.

This union of the whole human race, under certain univerfal laws, it may be faid, is not the partial, but the total and complete attainment of the grand aim, the final purpofe of Jurifprudence within the boundaries of mere Reafon. For, that the prototype of a juridical federation of men, according to public laws in general, muft be derived from Reafon *a priori*, is now obvious; fince all the examples, taken from experience, can indeed ferve the purpofe of illuftrating, but not of eftablifhing, the neceffity of a metaphyfical decifion of this important queftion. Thofe very men, who fmile at the novelty of this inquiry, incautioufly betray themfelves, when

they

they admit, and even make use of the common-place assertion, "that that is the best constitution, in which the laws govern, not men." And what, 'says the author,' can be more sublime than this idea, which is evidently applicable to practice, and capable of being realized in experience, and which alone—provided it is not attempted to be brought about by means of revolutions, or the forcible overthrow of all erroneous establishments (for that would be the annihilation of all law and justice), but by gradual reform, according to fixed principles—leads by continual approximation to the supreme political good, A PERPETUAL PEACE.

XXX. (12.) *Metaphysische Anfangsgründe der Tugendlehre.* Metaphysical Elements of Ethics. 8vo. *Koenigsberg.* 1797.

With this publication Prof. Kant will probably conclude his systematic labours in the field of the Critical Philosophy. Though, on account of its very recent appearance, I have not yet obtained a copy of this work, among the books lately received from Germany; I can in some degree satisfy the curiosity of the reader, by stating the object of it, as abstracted from the general Introduction, which is premised to the preceding "Elements of Jurisprudence."

'Moral laws can only be so far valid as rules, if they can be established *a priori*, so that the necessity of them becomes evident. For the conceptions and judgments, relative to our actions and omissions, have no moral application at all, if they contain nothing further than what is learned from experience. And if we should even be misled to assume any data, from the latter source, as moral principles, we cannot avoid falling into the grossest and most destructive errors.

'If the doctrine of morals had no other aim than that of personal happiness, it would be absurd to search for principles *a priori*, in order to establish such a doctrine. For, however plausible it may appear, that Reason can perceive previous to experience, by what means man may arrive at the permanent enjoyment of the true pleasures of life, yet every proposition of this kind, *a priori*, is either tautological, or it rests upon groundless hypotheses. Experience

perience alone can inform us of what is attended with pleasure. The natural instinct for nourishment, the sexual impulse, rest, motion, and (after developing the dispositions of nature) the struggles for honour, the enlargement of our knowledge, and the like, can intimate to every individual in particular, how he may *estimate* his pleasures, and at the same time inform him of the means, by which he is to *attain* them. All plausible reasoning *a priori* is, here, in reality nothing else but experience, which, by induction, has received a general character. This generality, far from being universal, is so very limited, that an indefinite number of exceptions must be granted to every individual, in order to adopt that choice in the mode of life, to his particular inclination, and to his susceptibility of pleasures;—so that, in the end, he can profit and grow wiser only from his own detriment, or that of others.

'The doctrines of morality, however, have a very different origin. They are imperative to every individual, without regarding his inclinations; for this reason merely, because he is a free subject, and is capable of reasoning practically. Instruction, in the laws of morality, is not derived from reflection upon ourselves and our animal nature, nor from the observation of the course of the world, namely from events and actions; but Reason itself commands us, how to act, though we should find no analogy or example in experience, corresponding with the present case. Reason, further, in this injunction, does not attend to the advantage or disadvantage, which may accompany our actions; for experience alone could give us any information upon this point. We are indeed entitled to pursue our advantage in every possible manner, provided that we act consistently with both Reason and prudence; for the former enjoins, while the latter only advises that, upon the whole, we shall derive greater advantages, if we follow, than if we transgress the dictates of Reason.'

The following Essays, written by Prof. Kant, were published in different periodical works of Germany, in the chronological order here stated.

1. *Von den verschiedenen Raçen der Menschen.* Of the different races of man. Published in ENGEL's *Philosopher of the world*: first Edit. 8vo. *Leipzig*, 1777, from p. 125 to p. 164.

2. *Briefwechsel zwischen Kant und dem verstorbenen Lambert.* Correspondence between Kant and the late Lambert.—Published in BERNOUILLI's *Literary Correspondence between learned Germans.* Vol. I. from p. 333 to 368.—1781.

3. *Idee zu einer allgemeinen Geschichte in weltbürgerlicher Absicht.*—Plan of a general history in a cosmopolitical view. Published in the *Berlin Monthly Magazine*, for November, 1784.

4. *Beantwortung der Frage: was ist Aufklärung?*—Reply to the question, what is understood by illumination (of mind). *Ibid.* for December, 1784.

5. *Ueber die Vulkane im Monde.*—On the Volcanos in the moon. *Ibid.* for March, 1785.

6. *Von der Unrechtmäßigkeit des Büchernachdrucks.*—On the injustice of printing spurious editions of books.—*Ibid.* for May, 1785.

7. *Beſtimmung des Begriffs einer Menſchenrace.*—Definition of the idea connected with the expreſſion "a race of men."—*Ibid.* for November, 1785.

8. *Muthmaſslicher Anfang der Menſchengeſchichte.*—On the probable Origin of Human Hiſtory. *Ibid.* for January, 1786.

This Eſſay the author himſelf conſiders as the moſt ſucceſsful of his popular productions, or minor works. And though I have not been able to procure a copy of that number, in which it appeared in the Berlin Monthly Magazine, without ordering the whole ſet for the year 1786, I can give the following character of this treatiſe, upon the authority of *Prof.* Will *of Altdorf*, as extracted from his "*Lectures on the Kantian Philoſophy*, 8vo. 200 pages; 1788," in which he ſays, p. 32:—' This maſterly perfor-
' mance contains a philoſophical explanation, which certainly is bet-
' ter founded than upon mere conjecture (as the title modeſtly ex-
' preſſes). Though it apparently deviates from the Moſaic nar-
' rative, it nevertheleſs forms an uſeful addition to the Bible, and
' affords illuſtrations of its hiſtorical truth.'

9. *Was heiſst: ſich im Denken orientiren?*—What is underſtood by the expreſſion, "to familiarize oneſelf in thinking;" i. e. to trace the ideas of our own mind to their ſource.—*Ibid.* for October, 1786.

10. *Abhandlung von dem Gebrauche teleologiſcher Principien in der Philoſophie.*—A Treatiſe concerning the application of teleological principles in philoſophy.—Publiſhed in the *German Mercury*, for January and February, 1788.

11. *Ueber das Mifslingen aller philosophischen Versuche in der Theodicee.*—On the failure of all philosophical attempts made in the Theodicea (by Leibnitz).—*Berlin Monthly Magazine* for September, 1791.

12. *Ueber das radikale Böse in der menschlichen Natur*—On the radical evil in human nature.—*Ibid.* for April, 1792.

13. *Ueber den Gemeinspruch: Das mag in der Theorie richtig seyn, taugt aber nicht für die Praxis.*—On the common-place assertion, "that may be true in theory, but is not applicable to practice." *Ibid.* for September, 1793.

14. *Etwas über den Einfluss des Mondes auf die Witterung.* Some Remarks relative to the influence of the Moon on the Weather. *Ibid.* for May 1794.

GLOSSARY

GLOSSARY.

Those terms, which explain themselves from the context of the Elements, are here omitted.

Such phrases, as have only one definition attached to them, must be understood in a general sense.

If any words occur in these definitions, which appear obscure or paradoxical, or do not sufficiently explain the meaning of the term under consideration, the reader is requested to have recourse to the further explanations of such words, in the alphabetical order of this Glossary.

To render this nomenclature subservient to the purpose of obtaining a more general view of Kant's Philosophy, than could be given in the preceding Elements, I have added explanations of many terms, which, though not occurring in this concise account, are used by the author in a peculiar sense.

Aesthetic

commonly signifies the Critique of Taste, but with Kant, the science containing the rules of sensation, in contradistinction to Logic, or the doctrine of the Understanding.

To Affect

means, to make immediate impressions on the Sensitive Faculty, i. e. to occasion representations and desires.

Affirmative, See Judgments.

Agreeable, (jucundum) *angenehm*,

is an object of the Sensitive Faculty, so far as it influences the will; or what pleases the senses in relation to feelings; or what affords us pleasure. The agreeable is not something *absolutely good*, i. e. good in the estimation of every rational being; because it does not immediately depend on Reason itself, but on the relative state of the mind, sensitive inclinations, and the like. The *good*, on the contrary, is an object of pure Reason, something that is conformable to the subject of all rational beings.

ANALYSIS—*Zergliederung*,

1) of an *idea*, is the reduction of it to those characters, of which it is compounded, in order to render the cognition of it clearer, though we cannot by this process make it more complete: hence it does not furnish us with additional knowledge, but merely arranges what we already possess.

2) considered in a *general sense*; Analysis is the science, treating of the form of real knowledge, and of the rules, by which we can examine that knowledge. It is a part of general *Logic*, and the negative criterion of truth; in this sense it is opposed to *Dialectic*.

3) *Transcendental Analysis* is the decomposition of the pure intellectual faculty into the elements, through which all the operations of thought are carried on.

4) of *pure practical Reason*, i. e. of the pure practical faculty of Reason, or of the pure will, into its elements.

ANALYTICAL, See JUDGMENTS.

ANTHROPOLOGY

signifies in general the experimental doctrine of the nature of man; and is divided, by Kant, into

1) *theoretical* or empirical doctrine of mind, which is a branch of Natural Philosophy;

2) *practical*, applied, and empirical Philosophy of Morals; Ethics—the consideration of the moral law in relation to the human will, its inclinations, motives, and to the obstacles in practising that law.

GLOSSARY.

ANTHROPOMORPHISMUS

is the art of attributing properties, observed in the world of sense, to a being remote from that world; or the sensualization of an idea of Reason: for instance, if we think of the Deity by human predicates.

ANTICIPATION

of experience, is a cognition of objects liable to observation *a priori*, previous to the observation itself, i. e. according to the pure form of perception, in consequence of which all phenomena are in *Space* and *Time*.

ANTINOMY OF REASON

1. in general; a contradiction between two laws;
2. in particular,

   a) of *pure speculative Reason*, is the contradiction in the results of it, in the application of its subjective idea relative to the unconditional thing, as well as in the application of its law, to the world of sense; a law, by which we form conclusions from the given (perceived) conditional thing, to what is unconditional.

   b) of *pure practical Reason*, which occurs in the inquiry into the highest good; where, on the one hand, practical Reason presupposes a necessary combination between virtue and happiness; but, on the other hand, there is no possibility of perceiving this combination analytically or synthetically, neither *a priori* nor *a posteriori*.—This antinomy is solved by showing the real connection between our good conduct and wellbeing; though this connection be concealed in the world of sense, yet it is really existing throughout the whole of it, and founded on the supersensible existence of ourselves, in connection with other things.

APODICTICAL

GLOSSARY.

APODICTICAL

or absolute, and attended with the consciousness of necessity.

A POSTERIORI,

i. e. through sensation, experience — The distinction between our knowledge obtained *a posteriori*, may be rendered more clear by its opposite, *a priori*. This distinction, in the philosophy of Kant, does not relate to the *series of time*, in which, but to the *source*, from which we receive knowledge or cognitions. Every representation or cognition is *a posteriori*, that is not founded merely on the original faculty of the mind, but in some one or other modification, which that faculty has received. Such representations or cognitions are therefore called *empirical*.

A PRIORI

originally does not signify, with KANT, a cognition or representation which, in order of time, precedes experience; of which we could become conscious independent of all sensations; and which, at the same time with the representing faculty, could be present in our mind as a real representation. Such are the " innate notions or ideas," which Kant expressly rejects throughout his works. But by the term " *a priori*" he understands those representations, which we acquire through the exertions of our own mind, or the thinking subject; and not *through* observation and sensation (*a posteriori*); not through given objects and from them, but *from* our faculty of cognition; though this latter must be rendered active by means of sensible impressions; and though the origin or production of such a representation can in this manner only be accomplished. Further, all that is *a priori*, which lies in the original conformation of the thinking subject, and is not founded on the operation of objects, which consequently is not first introduced *into* the mind, but is evolved *from* it, by

GLOSSARY. 143

its peculiar faculties. All thefe reprefentations neverthelefs prefuppofe experience, i. e. materials of application, if we are to become confcious of them, and refer them to objects. Without experience, they are non-entities. They do not precede experience as real reprefentations, but as the conditions, that render experience itfelf poffible. All objective reality of them is founded merely on experience.

APPERCEPTION

or confcioufnefs, or the faculty of becoming confcious, fignifies

1) in general, the fame as reprefentation, or the faculty of reprefenting;

2) in particular, the reprefentation as diftinct from the fubject that reprefents, and from the object that is reprefented.

3) *felf-confcioufnefs*, for which we have two faculties,

   a—the *empirical*, the internal fenfe, i. e, the confcioufnefs of our ftate at any time, of our obfervations. This is as fubject to change, as the obfervations themfelves; confidered in itfelf, it is not confined to any one place, and does not relate to the identity of the fubject.

   b—the *tranfcendental*, pure, original, i. e. the confcioufnefs of the identity of ourfelves, with all the variety of empirical confcioufnefs. It is that felf-confcioufnefs, which generates the bare idea " *I*," or " *I think,*" as being the fimple correlate of all other ideas, and the condition of their unity and neceffary connection.

There occurs a remark in Kant's Critique of pure Reafon, which is very humiliating in the tranfcendental doctrine of mind. He fays upon this occafion: " Though " confcioufnefs has no extenfive magnitude, and there- " fore is not divifible, it certainly has intenfive magni- " tude, and we may well conceive a ceffation of it, by a " *remiffion* of power.—For there is a certain degree of
" con-

"consciousness even in obscure representations, save that it does not always suffice to distinguish one idea from another, i. e. to make it clear and evident."

APPETITIVE FACULTY, or FACULTY OF DESIRING,

(*Begehrungsvermögen*)

in the most general sense, is the power inherent in a living being, to become through his representations the real cause of obtaining the objects corresponding with them; although the physical powers should not be adequate to the real production of the object desired: v, g. to wish for the great prize in the lottery, and the like.

APPREHENSION

is an act of the mind, by which the variety of individual perceptions is collected, combined with one another, and images are produced. We may distinguish,

1. the *pure synthesis of apprehension*, which compounds the variety of perceptions *a priori*, of Space and Time, and produces pure images, such as representations of numbers, geometrical figures, &c.

2. *empirical apprehension*, which combines the pure perceptions together with their matter, i. e. with sensible impressions, and produces the images of phenomena; v. g. when I observe a house, the freezing of water, &c.

APPROBATION, See SATISFACTION.

ARCHITECTONIC

is the art of constructing Systems. The Architectonic of pure Reason is, therefore, the plan for a System of pure philosophy.

ART, (*Kunst*)

1, in the most extensive sense, is arbitrary production, in consequence of preceding representations;

2, in a more limited sense, is production through Liberty, i. e. through a free will, which adopts Reason as the ground of its actions.

ARTICULATION

is the structure of the members of a science, or the systematic unity of it.

ASSERTORY, See IMPERATIVE and JUDGMENTS.

ATTRIBUTE

or *property*, is a character belonging to the existence of a thing conceived, as to its internal possibility; which character can be derived from things, or beings, as the necessary, i. e. sufficiently established consequence of them.

AUTONOMY,

a peculiar legislation of the *will*, is that constitution of a rational will, by which it is a law to itself, by which it determines itself, uninfluenced by inclinations. It is the independence of the will on all matter of it, i. e. on sensitive desires and their objects; the dependence on a rational will, merely on itself, i. e. upon the form of Reason. This is a practically necessary idea, in order to comprehend in this manner the possibility of an unconditional Imperative, and a goodness (morality) of actions independent on external interest.

AXIOM

is a synthetical principle *a priori*, which contains immediate or intuitive certainty; i. e. derived from objects of pure perception, and which does not admit of proof, and of the truth of which, we can point out no more accurate character, than what it itself expresses.

BAD—*Böses*

is that which, according to a rational principle, is a necessary object of detestation, in distinction from the *disagreeable*, i. e. what occasions an immediate sensation of pain.

Beautiful—*Schön*

is that, which excites pleasure and claims our approbation, without satisfying any wants: which pleases us by the harmonious employment of our representing faculty, unconnected with animal desires; and which we are fond of communicating to others; for instance, a witty idea, an acute or bold reflection, a strong picture, and the like.

Beauty——*Schönheit*

is the regular conformation of an object, so far as we observe this in it, without representing to ourselves any design or purpose; the regular *subjective* conformation of an object of nature or art; the expression of aesthetical ideas.

Being——*Wesen, Ding*

signifies 1) a conception with its constituent parts; logically, a *subjectum quod*. The term 'being' is distinguished from the word 'nature;' in as much as the former is the internal principle of all those determinations, which relate to the *possibility* of a thing; and the latter, nature, is the internal principle of all the determinations, relating to the *existence* of a thing:— 2) a real being, *subjectum quo*, the nature of a thing.

Belief—*Glaube*

1, signifies the *act* of taking something for true, on account of sufficient subjective, without any objective, reasons for doing so; or, in other words, to conceive things as subjects of cognition, or to admit their possible existence; because Reason enjoins it. These subjective grounds are a certain interest, certain *purposes*;—

2, the *habit*, the moral way of thinking, by which Reason considers as true, what is inaccessible to our theoretical cognition of things;—

3, in particular, *fides sacra*; the adoption of religious principles.

Canon,

CANON,

in general, means 'a science treating of the proper use of our faculty of cognition:' it is therefore opposed to '*Discipline*,' which is a guide, directing us to prevent the improper use of that faculty.

CATEGORICAL, See JUDGMENTS.

CATEGORIES

1, in general, are original notions or intellectual conceptions, which correspond with the simple form of a judgment; logical functions applied to objects in general;—

2, in particular, and according to their twofold use, they are,
  a) *Categories of theoretical Reason*, or of *Nature*; so far namely, as they are referred to the variety of sensible perceptions, in order to give it unity of apperception in a judgment of experience, or a cognition of nature; hence they are conceptions of unity in this cognition;
  b) *Categories of practical Reason*; so far as the same functions of the Understanding are referred to the variety of desires, in order to obtain for it unity in the rational idea of morality.

CAUSALITY—CAUSATION,

dependence, causal connection, signifies

1, *logically*, the function of the Understanding in a hypothetical judgment; the representation concerning the logical relation of cause and effect to one another;

2, as the *pure category* corresponding with this function, it expresses the notion of a real relation of different objects to one another; the necessary determination of the existence of a something through something of a different kind, whether this be homogeneous or not;—a species of synthesis, in which, according to, and by means of, something A (cause) we necessarily admit something very different, B (effect), and this in consequence of an absolutely general rule, so that we can conclude the existence of A, from the existence of B.

CERTAINTY—*Gewiſsheit*

is the consciousness arising from sufficient objective reasons, which are valid with respect to every body.

CHANGE—*Veränderung*,

accidens, is the succession of different states, transition of a thing from one state to another; the co-existence of what is standing and steady in time, with that which changes; the connection of opposite predicates in one and the same object, but at different times, v. g. motion, i. e. a being and not-being of the same thing, in the same place, but at different periods of time.

COGNITION,—*Erkenntniſs*,

in general, is a whole of connected representations in one act of consciousness; or the determinate reference of given representations to one object.—Every cognition has 1) *matter*, substance, i. e. something objective, which arises from the objects represented; the variety of given perceptions, objects: 2) *form*, i. e. a determinate way or mode, in which the given matter is received, modified, and combined by the representing faculty; that, which relates to the operation of mind in our cognitions; that, which depends upon the constitution of the thinking subject, or of the Understanding and Reason.

COMMON SENSE—*Gemeinsinn*

is the faculty of determining what pleases or displeases, not through conceptions, but merely through feelings; yet this determination has general validity.

GLOSSARY.

To Conceive—*Begreifen*

is a function of Reason, as "*to understand*," i. e. to think of an object, is an act of the Understanding.

Conception—*Begriff*,

1, in the most extensive sense; is every production of the active representing faculty, by which variety, or the multifarious, is connected into unity:

2, in a more determined sense; is a general representation abstracted from a variety of intuitions, and is opposed to a single representation or intuition. A conception of this kind is called by Kant, '*discursive*;' because it does not immediately refer to the object, but only by the representation of a character, which may be common to an infinite variety of things, the representation of which is contained *under* (not, *in*) a *discursive conception*.

In Concreto,

i. e, in real nature, in real objects of experience. Here, many things may be differently constituted, from what they are "*in abstracto*," i. e, when we reflect merely upon the pure idea of a thing, without attending to what may yet lie in the sensible perception of an object.

Condition—*Bedingung*,

the requisite, the ground, that which must be presupposed, in order to understand or to comprehend some other datum, or given thing.—Whatever presupposes a condition, is called *conditionate* or *conditional*.

In *practical* philosophy, we must distinguish

1, that, which is *practically conditionate*, which is determined through natural inclinations and necessities; for instance, the *imperatives* of happiness are valid only under the condition,

that

that a person feels an inclination for something, an impulse towards something, a necessity of a certain kind; and not otherwise:

2, that, which is *practically unconditionate*, which depends merely on Reason itself, i. e. on the moral law, for instance a pure, disinterested integrity, fidelity, and general utility.

Conformation—*Zweckmäſsigkeit*,

i. e. *forma, sive nexus finalis*, is that constitution of an object (or even of a state of mind, or of an action), which can be conceived, or thought of by us, as possible only through a causality according to conceptions, that is, through a Will.

Conscience—*Gewiſſen*,

means 1) the moral sense, relative to our own actions;
2) the self-determining moral faculty of judging; that unconditionate consciousness of duty, by which we can determine within ourselves, whether an action, we are about to perform, be just or otherwise.

Consciousness——*Bewuſtseyn*; See Apperception.

Constitution of State—*Staatsverfaſſung*;

the most perfect is that, in which the liberty of every individual is thoroughly consistent with the freedom of all members of society.

Constitutive

principles are those, which refer to an object, so as to determine something relative to it, i. e. to the representation of it; namely either the intuition of an object, v. g. the mathematical principles; or the experimental conception of it, v. g. the dynamical principles of the Understanding.

Regulative principles, on the contrary, are those, which

do not determine the objects themselves, but which afford us rules, i. e. determinations of the Understanding, to search for the objects in question.

To Construct

an idea, means to determine an individual object, i. e. the perception itself of that object, which is perfectly conformable to the general idea.

An object requires perception; an empirical perception, however, we cannot spontaneously produce; for the pure perception only is possible *a priori*. In this, namely Space and Time, we can form certain determinations, and combine them in the pure representing faculty, for instance an equilateral triangle. In a similar manner, we can construct the intensive magnitude of the sensations of the solar light, i. e. we can compound them of about 200,000 times the quantity of the light of the moon, and predicate them in a determined manner a priori;—of two given members of a proportion, we are able to construct a third, such as 2 : 4 : 8, &c.

Construction, in a general sense, signifies every exhibition of a general idea, by means of the self-active production of a perception, that corresponds with the idea.

Contact—*Berührung*,

1, in a *mathematical* sense, is the common boundary of two spaces, which is neither within the one nor the other, v. g. two intersecting lines do not touch one another, because their common point belongs to each of them:

2, in a *physical* sense, is the reciprocal effect of the repelling powers in the common boundary of two spaces; the immediate action and reaction of impenetrability. It is distinguished from the action at distance, i. e. from the effect of one matter upon the other, without the mediation of other intervenient matters through the empty space, v. g. in the essential attraction.—The beginning of contact in the approach of one matter to another, is called 'percussion' (*Stoſs*); the continuation of it, 'pressure' (*Druck*).

CONTINUANCE, or PERMANENCY—*Beharrlichkeit*, is existence at all times, without origin and evanescence. If, in this manner, we represent to ourselves the existence of phenomena, we class them under the pure intellectual conception, or Category of Substance.

CONTINUITY—*Stätigkeit*, refers to that magnitude, no part of which is the absolutely smallest and most simple, and in the solution of which we never can arrive at determined last unities; for instance, Space and Time, together with the phenomena that exist in them.

CONTRADICTION—*Widerspruch*; the principle of contradiction, i. e. "no one thing admits of being represented by contradictory predicates," is the negative criterion of all abstract truth, and the source of all our analytical, but not of synthetical, cognitions.

CONVICTION: See PROOFS.

COSMOLOGY;
the *transcendental*, rational cosmology; is either the Science embracing the whole of the phenomena in nature, or the metaphysical philosophy of the supersensible properties of all objects existing.

COSMO-THEOLOGY
is the cognition of a primitive Being, from the existence of a world in general, and its accidentality, as opposed to substance.

CRITICISM,
with Kant, signifies a critical mode of proceeding (doubts or delay) i. e. the maxim of general distrust with respect to all
synthetical

synthetical judgments *a priori*, until we have acquired a view of the universal ground of their possibility, in the essential conditions of our faculties of cognition.

CRITIQUE OF PURE REASON,

or transcendental Critique, is the Science of the pure faculty of Reason; the inquiry into those particulars, which Reason is able to know and to perform, from its own sources, and independent of experience;—*vid.* the more ample definition, pp. 42 and 43.

CULTURE,

in a *positive* sense, is used by Kant, to express the promptness we acquire in obeying rules; to which he opposes the term 'Discipline,' in a *negative* sense, which weakens and destroys that readiness, and makes us suspend our judgment. The whole Critique is a Discipline, as to the contents of pure rational cognition; but as to its method, only a particular part of the Critique is Discipline.

DAEMONOLOGY

is the doctrine of higher, but in other respects finite, beings resembling man; in opposition to *Theology*, the doctrine of the highest and infinite Being. Physical Teleology leads us to the former; moral Teleology to the latter.

DECEPTION—*Betrug, Täuschung,*

is that illusion of the *senses*, when we consider something, which is obtained by conclusions, as the immediate observation itself. This is no error of the senses, but of the Judging Faculty or the Understanding.—There is not only a deception of the *external sense*, v. g. the optical, but also, an illusion of the *internal sense*, v. g. when the fanatic believes to feel supernatural influence, or when we confound the sensation, which necessarily accompanies a moral action or determination of the will, with the cause of the action itself.

DEDUCTION,

in general, is the proof of a legal claim, a right; but, in particular, Kant understands by it the establishment of a representation; the proof of the right we have to make use of it; the proof, that a representation has sense, meaning, reality, objective validity, that it is not vague or empty, but relates to objects.

DEMONSTRABLE,

in *Logic*, are called those positions, which admit of immediate proof; in opposition to *indemonstrable* positions, that admit of no proof;—in a *critical* sense, such conceptions or judgments are demonstrable, as can be exhibited in perception, whether pure or empirical; in opposition to the *indemonstrable*, which cannot be thus exhibited.

DETERMINATION—*Bestimmung*,

1) as opposed to substance; accidens, a *logical predicate* of a subject: 2) a *real predicate*, which amplifies the conception; the determination of a thing: v. g. hard, elastic, &c. and *not* mere existence.—The *determinations* of a thing are, according to the source of cognition, *empirical*, when they are derived from experience; *transcendental*, when they arise from the representing subject *a priori*.

DETERMINISM

is the principle of determining the will from sufficient internal (subjective) reasons. To combine this principle with that of freedom, i. e. absolute spontaneity, occasions no difficulty.

DIALECTIC

is used by Kant in the following significations:
1) *logical*, formal; that Logic, which treats of the sources of error and illusion, and the mode of detecting them:

2)

2) *transcendental*, material Dialectic; the exhibition and judgment of that illusion, which arises from the subjective constitution of Reason itself a priori.

DISCIPLINE—*Zucht*, See CULTURE.

DISJUNCTIVE; See JUDGMENTS.

TO DISPUTE

upon any thing, means to decide it by proofs, i. e. from objective conceptions, on which the judgment is founded.—To *contest* (streiten) any thing, signifies to claim the consent of others to our judgment; though we cannot always produce objective reasons, and frequently have only subjective grounds to go upon, i. e. aesthetical grounds, feelings.

DISTANCE: See CONTACT.

DIVINES—*Geistliche*

are teachers of the pure moral Religion; as being opposed to 'priests, i. e. the consecrated ministers of *pious* customs and ceremonies.

DOGMA,

or a dogmatical judgment, is a direct synthetical decision from conceptions, and is distinguished

1, from analytical judgments, which properly teach nothing;

2, from experimental positions, which have no apodictic or demonstrative certainty;

3, from mathematical principles, i. e. from synthetical judgments arising from the construction of ideas; and

4, from principles, i. e. indirect synthetico-apodictic judgments, such as the principle of the '*sufficient reason*.' Speculative pure Reason contains no dogmas; for its ideas have no constitutive, objective reality; hence it admits of no dogmatical method.

Dogmatism

or the dogmatical process of pure Reason, is the prejudice of maintaining and deciding metaphysical propositions according to customary principles, and of determining upon the existence or non-existence of supersensible objects and their properties, without having previously deduced the possibility of them from the faculties of Reason: it is therefore, Metaphysics without a previous Critique.—Dogmatism paves the way for Scepticism; this compels us to have recourse to a Critique; and this lastly conducts us to a solid system of science.

Duty—*Pflicht*,

is the obedience of a law from a true regard for it; the objective necessity of an action for the sake of the law, so far as this *obliges* the will, i. e. *morally* compels it; though it may have some other subjective desires.

Dynamical

1) in general, is said of things, so far as we do not attend to their quantity in perception, but to the ground or cause of their existence. Hence Kant calls, 2) in particular, a *synthesis* dynamical, where the things combined necessarily belong to one another, but must not necessarily be of a homogenous nature, because they do not, (as in the *mathematical* synthesis) constitute together One magnitude, *quantum*. The synthesis of cause and effect, for instance, is dynamical.

Effect: See Causality.

Empirical: See A posteriori.

Epigenesis of pure Reason

has been called the Kantian explanation concerning the coincidence of the pure intellectual conceptions (Categories) with the objects of experience; according to which explanation,

by

by these pure notions or conceptions, being the forms of thought, experience itself and its objects, as such, become possible.

Vid. the fourth Problem, p. 49 & seq.

ETHICO-THEOLOGY

is that species of Theology, which is derived from pure moral arguments, and admits no symbolical representations.

EXPERIENCE—*Erfahrung*

is, with Kant, an objective, i. e. universally valid and necessary synthetical cognition of given objects (phenomena); or, the representation of observations in a necessarily determined connection; cognition through combined observation; the connection of sensible representations according to certain laws.

EXTENSION—*Ausdehnung*,

in the most comprehensive sense, is the representation of a whole, by means of its continued parts. If these are simultaneous or coexistent, it is *Space*: if they follow one another in succession, it is *Time*. According to this use of the word 'extension,' every *magnitude* is called *extensive*, which is represented by the successive connection of parts of time and space, when the representation of the whole becomes possible only by the representation of the parts. In this sense extension is used in Mathematics, and hence the *mathesis extensorum*.

EXTENSIVE POWER

is, according to Kant, original elasticity or the power of an extended thing by means of the repulsion of all its parts.—It so far differs from what is commonly called *elasticity*, as this is the power of a matter, to resume its form or magnitude changed by another moving power, upon the remission of the latter.

FANCY

Fancy—*Wahn*

is that deception, in which we consider the mere representation of a thing as equivalent to the thing itself. *Religious fancy* manifests itself in this, when man considers the statutory belief and ceremonies as the substance of religion, and as the supreme condition, upon which he may obtain the approbation of the Deity.

Fatalism

is that system, in which the connection of purposes in the world is considered as accidental; and in which this connection is yet derived from a Supreme Being, not indeed from his rational nature, but from the necessary constitution of this Being, and the unity of the world thence arising. Such, for instance, is the system of Spinoza.

Final purpose—*Endzweck*

is that, which requires no other purpose as the condition of its possibility; which contains in itself the determining cause, the necessary and sufficient condition of all other purposes.

Form

is the determined mode of thinking something, or the manner of its existence; it is opposed to *matter*, i. e. that which is given and determinable.

Function

is the office, the activity, the form of an higher faculty of cognition; 1) of the *Understanding* —to think and to judge; 2) of *Reason* —to conclude.

Function is opposed to *affection*, as this implies a change, to which our Sensitive Faculty is subject.

Genius—*ingenium*

is the talent, the gift of nature, or the native disposition of the mind, from which nature prescribes the rule to art.

To Give—*Geben*

an object, is to perceive it, to observe it; to refer the conception of it to real or possible experience. That an object be given, is a necessary condition for receiving a *cognition* of it, but not so, for *thinking* of it only.

Good—*Gutes*,

is that, of which reason approves, and which it considers as practically necessary; that, which according to a rational principle is a necessary object of the faculty of desiring; which has some value. It is opposed to the *agreeable*, which satisfies the inclinations of the senses, or which affords us pleasure.

Gravitation

is called the effect of universal attraction, which every part of matter immediately exerts on all other parts, and at all distances.—Kant distinguishes *gravitation* from *gravity*, i. e. the effort of matter to move itself in the direction of the superior gravitation.

Ground of Determination—*Bestimmungsgrund*.

The grounds or causes of determining our actions, are called *formal* (laws), so far as they ascertain the way and manner, in which we view an object; *material* (maxims), so far as they determine the objects, to which an action is directed, *subjective* (laws), so far as they depend upon pure rational conceptions; *objective* (motives), so far as they affect the Sensitive Faculty; *practical*, so far as the last ground, which determines the will is an idea from pure Reason; *aesthetical*, when the last grounds of volition are met with in certain feelings of sense. The pure moral law is the formal ground of determining moral actions; hence the good and bad, i. e. the objects of moral desire and aversion, depend upon this law: it is, therefore, likewise the material ground of determination,

tion, and is objective, as being the form of practical Reason itself. The moral sense is the subjective ground of the same action; but, as this sense or feeling itself is again produced by Reason, it cannot be aesthetical.

Happiness—*Glückseligkeit*

signifies, with Kant, the whole prosperity of a finite, rational being; the consciousness of the agreeable situation, which uninterruptedly accompanies the whole existence of such a being.—It arises from the satisfaction of all inclinations, from the attainment of all ends, which the Sensitive Faculty proposes, and is therefore a prototype of the imagination.

Heteronomy,

or a foreign legislation, is that, in which not the will itself, but something else determines us to act in a certain manner; when not the action itself, but merely its object, its effect, interests us; when, beside the idea of the action, another extraneous allurement or compulsion, i. e. hope or fear must concur, in order to produce the action.

Highest Good—*Höchstes Gut*

is the whole unconditionate object of pure practical Reason, and consists 1) in virtue as the constituent of being happy; the *supreme good*; 2) in happiness itself, so far as it is connected with that worth; the *perfect good*.

Hypothesis

is an explanation of something that is real, by something else, the reality of which is not demonstrable or, at least, is not demonstrated.

Hypothetical: See Judgments.

Idea.

This expression Kant employs more determinately (borrowed

rowed from Plato), than is commonly used in modern languages. According to Kant, it signifies a necessary conception of Reason, the object of which cannot be perceived by the senses, nor acquired by experience.

IDEALISM

is called that system of philosophy, in which the external reality of certain intuitive representations is disputed or doubted, and space as well as external objects are asserted to be mere fancies.—Such is the system of the celebrated bishop Berkley.

ILLUSION—*Täuschung, Schein,*

is a false judgment, in which we attribute a predicate to an object in itself, which predicate belongs to it merely in relation to the subject.

IMAGINATION—*Einbildungskraft*

is the faculty of representing an object, in perception, though it should not be present.

IMMANENT

is used by Kant in opposition to *transcendental*: the former term is applied to conceptions or principles, which are valid in nature, and are used concerning objects of experience, phenomena; though the principles themselves are not derived from experience: v. g. the application of the principle of causality is *immanent*, when it is applied to the relation subsisting among the phenomena of nature as such: it would be *transcendent*, when we go with this principle beyond experience, and endeavour to prove from it the existence of the Deity.

IMMORTALITY—*Unsterblichkeit,*

of the soul, cannot be proved from speculative reasons, nor from its self-subsistence, simplicity, and so forth; hence it is not

not properly an object of knowledge, but it may yet be concluded by analogy, partly from the disproportion of the great talents of man to the confined duration of his present life; and partly for the sake of giving energy to the necessary laws of morality: in this manner it may be defended against all the speculative objections of the rude materialists.

IMPERATIVE—*Gebot,*

1) in general, is an objective practical law;
2) in a more determined sense, it is the formula or prescribed model of that law, by which it is referred to a will, as the necessary precept of its actions; though this will may subjectively have some other object of its wishes, because it is not purely rational, but also depends on inclinations, v. g. those of the human species.

IMPRESSION—*Eindruck.*

'Objects make impressions upon us,' signifies with Kant, that objects of the external sense, external phenomena, affect the internal sense, and are real objects of thought; consequently, that they are sufficiently distinguished from the thoughts themselves, which never can be exhibited in *Space.*—The modus operandi or the origin of this influence occasioned by sensible impressions, cannot be explained by the principles of Kant, nor of any other philosopher.

INCLINATION—*Neigung*

signifies a sensible impulse, the dependence of the appetitive faculty on sensations; in opposition to '*interest,*' i. e. the dependence of that faculty on rational ideas.—The amount of all inclinations is *self-love*; the satisfaction or gratification of an inclination is *pleasure*; that of all inclinations, is *happiness.*

INDETERMINISM

is that inert system of philosophy, which imagines freedom to consist

consist in the accidentality (chance) of actions; that the will is not at all determined by arguments; and that a free being is equally liable, to commit good as well as bad actions

INDIFFERENTISTS

are called those latitudinarians of neutrality, who assert, that there are indifferent or involuntary actions, which are neither morally good nor bad.

INDIVIDUAL: See JUDGMENTS.

INDUCEMENT—*Bewegungsgrund*,

is the objective ground of the will, so far as it, being represented by Reason, determines the will.—It is distinguished from the 'MOTIVE,' *Triebfeder*, which is something subjective, i. e. an inclination, which impels us to an action.

INDUCTION

is cognition of the whole or of the genus, by means of the parts observed or perceived: v. g. if we ascribe to bodies in general, what we have hitherto every where discovered in them. From induction there arises only a comparative universality, or generality of an empirical rule.

INFINITE: See JUDGMENTS.

INTUITION—*Anschauung*,

1) in the most extensive sense, is every representation of variety or the multifarious, so far only, as we consider the variety, and not the unity in the object. In so far, however, as the representation presents variety, we may call every representation a perception, and unfold it further as such;

2) in a more confined and proper sense, an intuition is not a bare representation of sight, but every immediate representation of the individual thing, a single representation, which

immediately refers to an object, and by which this is given, i. e. perceived.

To Judge—*Urtheilen*

signifies to give unity to two representations, namely to the representation of an object, v. g. of a man, and that of a character, v. g. man is a rational being.

Judging Faculty—*Urtheilskraft*,

is the power of thinking of the particular, as contained under the general or universal.—Kant divides this Faculty into 1) the determining (subsuming) power of judging; this again is a) empirical, b) transcendental; 2) the reflecting or reflex power of judging, which is further subdivided into a) aesthetical, b) teleological.———The meaning of these terms may be found in their respective places in the alphabetical order.

Judgments—*Urtheile*,

according to the usual definition of Logicians, are representations of one relation subsisting between two notions or conceptions. This explanation, however, applies only to the categorical judgments, and does not determine the nature of this relation. For, even by the laws of the representing power, there arises likewise a relation among our conceptions, which cannot with any propriety be called a judgment. According to Kant, therefore, a judgment in general is the act of comprehending a variety or the multifarious, represented by an intuition, under objective unity. And as nothing else but intuitions can be represented under this unity, they must exhibit either properties of a thing, or effects of a thing, or parts of a whole. Hence the following Judgments will be the result of all representations.

I. Judgments of Quantity, which determine what can be comprehended under objective unity. The three species of them are,

Individual,

Individual or *singular*, when one individual thing,
Particular, when many,
Universal, when all,
} can be comprehended under objective unity.

II. JUDGMENTS OF QUALITY, which ascertain the manner, in which the act of comprehending can be carried on.

Their species are,

Affirmative, i. e. so as really to unite an intuition with a conception;

Negative, or so as to exclude something from a conception;

Infinite, or so as to exclude a whole class of intuitions, without determining thereby the conception in any degree.

III. JUDGMENTS OF RELATION, or such as express the relations subsisting between things and properties, causes and effects, parts and a whole. The species of this class are,

Categorical, when particular properties or things,

Hypothetical, when particular effects or causes,

Disjunctive, when particular parts or wholes are comprehended under objective unity.

IV. JUDGMENTS OF MODALITY, are those which denote the particular faculties of the mind, by means of which they have been formed; or determine that place, where the things judged of, or comprehended under objective unity, have their respective seat. The species of these are,

Problematical, when the things exist in the Understanding alone, or are mere ideas, of which it is not certain, whether they really exist without the mind;

Assertory, when the things comprehended under the objective are in reality conceived, and believed to correspond with the conception we have of them; and

Apodictical, or attended with the character of necessity, when the things are so conceived, as to carry along with them

them the conviction, that according to the constitution of the Understanding, they cannot be otherwise conceived, whether in an affirmative or negative instance.

The three last species of Judgments have been reduced by Kant to the class of 'modality;' because they add nothing to the contents of a judgment, as is the case with those of 'quantity,' 'quality,' and 'relation.'

The further division of Judgments, as to their *origin, objects, form, use,* &c. cannot be detailed in an elementary treatise; for this would require a separate work, which Kant has actually published, and of which the reader will find some account, in the preceding elementary view of his works, under No. XXV. (9).

To Know—*Wissen,*

objectively considered, is to have apodictical or demonstrative certainty. This is possible only in cognitions, the origin of which is *a priori*.

Knowledge: See Cognition.

Law—*Gesetz.*

A Law is an objective necessary rule, or the representation of a general condition, according to which a variety or what is multifarious must be uniformly applicable to all.

Legality—*Gesetzmässigkeit,*

moral rectitude, is predicable of every determination of the will and subsequent action, which agree with the moral law; whether this action arise from the representation of the law itself, or from the inclination resulting from the view of the success and advantage of the action.—As to the *morality,* i. e. the properly moral value of the action, there is still required a virtuous sentiment, or the determination to a lawful action through the law independent of any prospect of gain or loss.

LIBERTY

GLOSSARY.

LIBERTY, FREEDOM—*Freyheit*,

is confidered as the attribute of an intelligent being, fo far as its actions are not determined by foreign caufes. Such a caufality and its action is called free.

LIMITATION

is a Category of Quality, which is conceived in things, by connecting the predicate of reality with that of negation; in a fimilar manner as the judgments of quality (i. e. the fpecies of thofe called by Kant, *infinite*), have fomething common with the form of both, *affirmative* and *negative*.

MAN—*Menfch*

a moral being, fubject to moral laws by virtue of his rational nature: hence it is highly improper to call him a fighting animal, as fome of the modern court-philofophers are pleafed to define him.—A *bad* man, is he who has adopted deviation from the moral law as a maxim; a *good* man, who values the moral law as his fupreme maxim;—an *accomplifhed* man, who is both inclined and able to communicate his agreeable feelings to others;—a *man of good morals*, whofe actions correfpond with the moral law.

MATERIALISM

in general, is the affertion, that the whole of worldly beings confift of matter;—in particular, the *pfychological* materialifm, or the doctrine, that the perfonality of man can fubfift only under the condition of his being the fame body;—the *cofmological*, that the exiftence and prefence of the world can be owing to other circumftances, than to that of its being in Space.

MATTER,

1) as oppofed to *form*, is the given, perceived thing in general; that, which is determinable; the correlate of the determination:

tion: 2) in opposition to *mind*, i. e. an object of the internal sense, matter is that, which is determined by the form of external perception; the substance of bodies.

Maxims

are subjective principles of Reason, relative to free actions; whereas *laws* are the necessary objective rules, which apply with equal force to every individual, whether morally disposed to obey them, or not.

Mechanically

1) in general, is all that, which necessarily happens in time, according to the law of causality; 2) in particular, the effect, which bodies in motion produce upon one another by the communication of their motion (not by their internal powers, as in the chemical effects of bodies), v. g. mechanical separation by the wedge.

Mechanism of Nature

is the necessary consequence of events in time, according to the natural law of causality.

Metaphysics

1, as defined by Baumgarten, is the science treating of the first principles of human knowledge; it has no fixed limits, by which it is separated from other sciences:

2, with Kant; the whole system of pure philosophy; the philosophy of things that are not the objects of sense; or the Science of the hyperphysical predicates of sensible objects.

Method

1, *Theoretically*, is the mode of teaching; the form of a science; that process of arranging the variety in our cognitions under systematic unity, which is guided and determined by rational principles:

2, *practically*, the mode and way of establishing genuine moral principles. The *methodical doctrine of practical Reason* is, therefore, that part of the 'Critique of Reason,' which teaches this method from principles.

The *transcendental doctrine of method* is the science treating of the form of a metaphysical system.

MIND—*Seele*

signifies 1) the soul as phenomenon, as the object of the internal sense, with all the internal reflections: it is thus considered in the experimental doctrine of mind; 2) the transcendental subject of thoughts, which we can represent to ourselves merely through the consciousness accompanying all our representations; 3) in particular, this self-same being, as the vital principle of matter.

MODALITY: See JUDGMENTS.

MOTIVE—*Triebfeder*: See INDUCEMENT.

MYSTICISM—*Schwärmerey*

1) that of *speculative Reason*, is Plato's doctrine of intellectual perceptions, and the cognoscible reality of those pretended innate conceptions of things beyond the world of sense; v. g. if we attribute positive predicates to the Deity, and still dispute their borrowed origin from phenomena:

2) that of *practical Reason*, is the moral system, which does not derive the material ground of human actions from the world of sense, and which consequently establishes the morality of them upon supersensible perceptions.; v. g. if we admit such divine laws, as differ from the essential commands of Reason.

NECESSARY: See JUDGMENTS.

NECESSITY—*Nothwendigkeit*

1) *logical*, formal; the necessary connection of conceptions in

an apodictical Judgment; that necessity, according to which certain predicates belong to a certain conception: 2) *real*, material, physical necessity of existence; the impossibility of non-existence: 3) *moral*, practical necessity, which depends upon practical Reason.

NEGATIVE: See JUDGMENTS.

NOTION

is a pure intellectual conception, which arises from the act of referring the form of a judgment to an object.—An original (not, innate) notion is called a Category.

NOUMENON—*Ding an sich*,

an object or thing in itself, i. e. without or external to the mind in a transcendental sense; a thing exclusive of our representation. It is generally opposed to the term '*phenomenon*,' or the sensible representation of an object.

NUMBER—*Zahl*,

is the representation of unity, from the successive addition of One to One, which is of a similar species. By the idea 'number,' the Category of *Quantity* is sensualized, and the pure scheme of Quantity, or series of time exhibited.

OBJECT—*Gegenstand*

of a representation, in general, is the individual thing, to which the variety of given matter in a representation is referred.

OBJECTIVE

signifies, in general, every thing which has objective reality, which relates to an object of sense and experience.

OBLIGATION—*Nöthigung*

is a moral and practical determination of a will governed by rational motives; or the practical necessity of volition, in a

possible

possible contradiction to natural inclinations. In a sacred will, therefore, no obligation takes place.

ONTOLOGY

1) as it is pretended; a systematic doctrine of synthetical cognitions *a priori* of things in general:
2) as it is possible; a complete analysis of the pure Understanding, or transcendental philosophy, i. e. the science of the most general conceptions and laws of all rational and moral objects collectively considered;—in opposition to that part of Metaphysics, which treats of the particular objects of the internal or external sense.

ONTO-THEOLOGY

is the cognition of a Supreme Being from bare conceptions.

ORGANON

1) in general, is the knowledge of those rules, by which a scientific system can be constructed:
2) in particular, the *Organon of pure Reason*; i. e. an Organon for the purposes of Metaphysics. From the complete application of the Organon, arises a system of pure Reason.

ORIGIN—*Ursprung*,

the *first origin* is the derivation of an effect from its first cause, i. e. that cause, which is not again the effect of another cause of the same kind.

ORIGINALLY—*Ursprünglich*,

i. e. not derived; for instance, original action: (*See* CAUSALITY); an original character, which requires no derivation, no proof.

PARALOGISM

1) *logical*: a false conclusion of Reason, as to its form:
2) *transcendental*: when the ground of the paralogism depends

pends upon the constitution of the faculty of cognition itself, for instance, in the transcendental doctrine of mind.

PARTICULAR: See JUDGMENTS.

PATHOLOGICAL

is called that, which depends upon the passive part of human nature, upon the sensitive faculty. It is opposed to '*practical*,' i. e. that, which depends upon the free activity of Reason.

PEOPLE OF GOD

is a people, that live under the government of divine laws.

PERCEPTION

generally signifies the same as '*intuition*;' but, in particular, it is used by Kant in a more limited sense, i. e. a representation accompanied with consciousness or apperception.

PERMITTED—*Erlaubt*

1) is that, which corresponds with a barely possible practical precept; *non-permitted*, what militates against a problematical Imperative: 2) that, which is consistent with a general law of morality, with the autonomy of the will; the contrary is unpermitted. In the former signification, the *non-permitted* is distinguished from that, which is '*contrary to duty*,' or what is against a real, subsisting law. In the latter sense, these terms are equivalent to each other.

PHENOMENON: See NOUMENON.

PHILOSOPHER—*Weltweiser*,

in idea, is he who renders all cognitions subservient to the necessary purposes of human Reason; a legislator of that faculty; a master in the science of wisdom.

GLOSSARY.

To Philosophize

means to exercise one's peculiar talent in the philosophical use of Reason, i. e. in the explanation of that, which is explicable.

Physico-Theology

or rather physico-teleological theology, is the cognition of the Deity, as being the author of that order and perfection in the natural world of sense, which is every where discoverable.

Phoronomy

is the pure doctrine of the magnitude of motion.

Possibility—*Möglichkeit*

1) the form of a *problematical judgment*; the conceivable connection of two conceptions: 2) the corresponding pure *Category*, i. e. the reference of a form of thought in a problematical judgment, to perceptions in general, to an object: 3) the application of this Category to sensible perceptions; the agreement of a conception with the general form of sensible perceptions of time.—Impossibility, therefore, signifies the disagreement, the inconsistency with this form.

Practical

is that, which depends on freedom, on the self-active faculty of desiring; which relates to that faculty as the ground, consequence, &c.; for instance, practical cognition, laws, principles, philosophy.

Pragmatical

is that, which is designed for the promotion of general prosperity.

Praying—*Beten,*

is a mere declaration of wishes towards the Divine Being; a Being, that stands in need of no explanation of the internal sentiment of the wishing person.—Praying considered as the

means

means of producing effects upon God, is superstition. In order to improve ourselves, and to enliven our moral sentiments, it is one of the most salutary, but by no means generally necessary means.

Precept—*Vorschrift*

means a practical rule, in the most extensive sense, whether it have an absolute (lawful) or only a comparative universality.

Principle—*Grundsatz*

is every general cognition, from which others may be consistently derived and conceived.

Problematical: See Judgments.

Proofs—*Beweise*

1) in general, are objective grounds of conviction. To prove something, is to demonstrate it sufficiently from objective, logical reasons, to convince, or at least, to prepare the mind for conviction, and not merely to persuade, i. e. to cause or produce our approbation from subjective (aesthetical) grounds of determination: 2) in particular; proofs are either *empirical* from real experience; or *a priori*, from Reason and independent of all matter of experience.

Psychology,

is the doctrine of mind; the physiology of the internal sense, and a part of physics in general.

Pure—*rein*: See A Priori.

Purpose—*Zweck*,

in general, is the conception of an object, so far as it contains, at the same time, the ground of the reality of this object. A purpose is said to be *hypothetical*, when it presents itself as the

the means of attaining some other object; *categorical*, when it exhibits itself as final purpose in the opposite case.—*Purpose of Nature* is the exhibition of the idea of a real, objective conformity in nature. A thing exists as a purpose of nature, when it is of itself both cause and effect.

The science or philosophy of all purposes is called *Teleology*.

QUALITY,
QUANTITY, } See JUDGMENTS.

REALITY—*Wirklichkeit*

is real, not merely ideal existence; and this is conceived 1) *pure*, through that Category, which is founded upon the form of assertory judgments: 2) *sensualized*; i. e. the circumstance of being in a determined time.

REASON—*Vernunft*

A) *generally* implies the whole, supreme, self-active faculty of cognition, in contradistinction to the low, merely passive, faculty of the senses; and, in this view, the Understanding is likewise comprehended under it. Hence the whole faculty of cognitions *a priori* is called *pure Reason*; which is divided into the faculty of forming conceptions, i. e. the Understanding; and into the faculty of forming conclusions, i. e. Reason in a more limited sense.—

B) *in particular*: the power of conceiving something from principles; of apprehending the particular from the general; of reducing the unity of the rules of the Understanding to principles; of classing particular conceptions under those, which are general; and finally, of exerting the highest degree of activity in the free operating faculty of cognition.—Thus defined, Reason is not only distinguished from the Sensitive Faculty, but likewise from the Understanding in a more limited sense.

RECEPTIVITY,

the susceptibility of impressions; the power of receiving representations; of being affected by objects; the *passive* faculty of representation; sensibility. This, combined with spontaneity, forms the substance of the representing power of man.

REFLECTION—*Ueberlegung*,

1) *logical*; the comparison made between existing conceptions in general; 2) *transcendental reflection*, the mode of comparing representations with respect to the faculty of cognition, in which they are compared; the act of reflecting upon the manner, how and by what subjective conditions (states of mind) we arrive at certain conceptions and judgments, whether through inclination and custom, through the Sensitive Faculty, the Understanding, or through Reason.

REGULATIVE PRINCIPLES: See CONSTITUTIVE.

RELATION: See JUDGMENTS.

RELIGION

1) *subjectively* considered, is the representation of the essential laws of Reason, as the result of divine commands and of virtue; the coincidence of the will of a finite being with that of a sacred and beneficent author of the world, who has both, the will and power of realizing the most exact proportion between the happiness and the moral conduct of man. All Religion is founded upon morals. The Science of Religion is, therefore, called Moral Theology:
2) *objectively* considered, it is the whole compass of those doctrines, which relate to the subjective Religion.

REPRESENTATION—*Vorstellung*

is an internal determination, a modification of the mind. It is converted into a cognition, as soon as it is referred to an object.

RULES

Rule—*Regel*

is a conception or a judgment, so far as the connection of a variety is subjected to a general condition.—As to their validity, Rules are either *universal*, which are necessarily valid, and admit of no exception, for instance, the moral law, and all the rules a priori : or they are *general*, when we frequently observe them to be advantageous and applicable to the purposes of life : such are, for instance, the rules of prudence.

Satisfaction—*Wohlgefallen*

is the corresponding relation of an object to the sense of feeling, or to the subject itself.

Scepticism

of pure Reason, is the opinion, that we can form no decision upon the existence and non-existence of supersensible things and their properties, without pointing out with accuracy the grounds of this impossibility, which lie in the cognitive faculty itself.

Schema

1) is the general determination of a perception according to general ideas ; for instance, the sensible representation of a man, a horse, a house in general. It must, therefore, not be confounded with a 'picture,' i. e. an example in concreto, v. g. that of an individual or particular man, horse, house, &c. 2) the *transcendental* schema of a pure intellectual notion, is the pure and general sensualization of such a notion a *priori* ; the sensible condition, under which the pure notions of the intellect are used ; i. e. objects can be classed under it.—The regular succession of variety is apriori the schema of causality ; number in general is the schema of quantity ; whereas an individual number, as that of 5, 15, &c. is merely the picture of it.

Sensation—*Empfindung*

is sensible representation, impression of an actually present object upon the mind, modification of the Sensitive Faculty.

Sense, or Sensitive Faculty—*Sinnlichkeit*,

according to Kant, is that faculty of the mind, which is liable to be modified and affected by things, and thereby to receive impressions or representations of things. It is, therefore, neither a bare modification of the Understanding, as with Leibnitz, nor a mere activity or excitement of the corporeal organs, the peculiar existence of which, if it is to become an object of cognition, rather presupposes a receptivity in the mind itself.

The '*pure Sensitive Faculty a priori*,' implies the faculty in itself; that, which belongs to it as a power of susceptibility a priori, which is not first determined by the sensible impressions, but which rather determines the latter themselves, according to Space and Time; it is the subjective condition of all that, which receives by it (namely the Sensitive Faculty a priori) the character of reality.

Sensibility—*Empfindbarkeit*

is sometimes, though rarely, used in these 'Elements' instead of sensation; it expresses rather the capacity of receiving sensible impressions.

Sensible and Sensitive

must not be confounded with one another, as the former is analogous to sensibility, the latter to sensation.

Simultaneity—*Zugleichseyn*,

is the existence of a variety or the multifarious, at one and the same time.

Space—*Raum*

is the intuitive representation of things being without and near one another, and of extension in general.

Spontaneity

1) in general, is self-active, unconditionate causality;
2) in particular, the *spontaneity of the representing faculty* consists in the activity or operation of the representing subject upon the impressions received. The representing faculty is called, Understanding, Reason in the most extensive sense, so far only, as it is self-active and apprehends the impressions received, connects them into a whole, and has the power of reproducing them.

Spurious worship—*Afterdienst*

is such a fanciful veneration of the Deity, as is contrary to that true service, which he himself requires; v. g. by penance, mortification, pilgrimage, &c.

Subject

1) *logical*; that in general, in which certain predicates are inherent: 2) the *transcendental* subject in particular, the representing, thinking being in relation to its own thoughts: 3) the *real* subject, substance.

Subjective,

as opposed to *objective*, signifies 1) that, which belongs to the subject, i. e. all representations: 2) that, which in part at least is determined by the nature of the subject. This is likewise the case in all our representations: 3) that, which relates to no object corresponding with the representation; those conceptions and judgments, that cannot be exhibited in perception, as the Deity, Liberty, Immortality: 4) in a *practical* sense, such practical principles (maxims), which are not immediately founded upon Reason itself, but upon the particular constitution of the acting subject, upon the sensible impulse and inclinations of it.

Substance

1) according to the pure *Category*, a subject in a categorical

judgment; all that, which is not considered as predicate of something else: in this sense the mind itself is called substance: 2) *sensualized*; substance in a phenomenon, the continuance, perdurability in a perceived object, which exists at all times; that, which contains the ground of reality in the accidens, v. g. matter is the substance of all external objects, without which no object could be conceived in Space: 3) *Substance in itself*, external to the phenomenon; it is that unknown something, by which the different sensations are produced, and necessarily connected with one another in a phenomenon.

Substratum.

The *supersensible substratum* of nature is that object, of which we can determine nothing in an affirmative sense, save that it is a being in itself, of which we know merely the phenomenon.

Synthesis

1) in general, is the composition or combination of various representations (whether intuitions or conceptions) into one cognition, which may be conception, judgment, &c. 2) in particular: a) *pure* transcendental synthesis a priori, is the act of combining the variety of Space and Time into One representation of Space and Time. This lies at the foundation of pure Mathematics:—b) *empirical* synthesis, when any experimental varieties, i. e. sensations, are connected into unity. Each of these species consists of three varieties, namely,

1) the synthesis of *apprehension*, when the affections of our internal and external sense are apprehended and arranged;

2) the synthesis of *reproduction*, when that, which has been collected and connected, is reproduced by the power of imagination, in order that the preceding affections may be annexed to those immediately succeeding; and

3) the synthesis of *recognition*, which forms One Intuition of what has been apprehended and connected.

System

is a whole, which is connected by one principle, and therefore has necessary unity. It is opposed to '*aggregate*,' i. e. a whole, which owes its origin to the occasional or accidental addition of one part to another, and consequently has not the character of necessary completeness.

Technic

1) in a proper sense, means Art, causality according to ideas, purposes: 2) in a general sense, the *technic of nature*, the causality of nature in relation to those productions, which correspond with our conceptions of a purpose; in opposition to '*mechanism*,' i. e. the determination of causes according to the laws of motion.

Teleology: See Purpose.

Theology: See Religion.

Theosophy

signifies that theoretical cognition of the divine nature and existence, which satisfactorily explains the constitution of the world, as well as the moral laws.

Thing in itself : See Noumenon.

Time—*Zeit*

is, according to Kant, the original perceptive representation of the possibility of simultaneity and succession.

Totality—*Allheit*,

the representation of the whole, (*universitas*); that function of the Understanding, by which, when it is applied to conceptions, a plurality of cognitions is comprehended and connected into a general one; when applied to perceptions, Totality is nothing else than plurality considered in things as unity, and forms a species of a Category, viz. that of Quantity.

TRANSCENDENT—*überschwenglich*: See IMMANENT.

TRANSCENDENTAL,

in a general sense, signifies a representation (whether perception or conception), a judgment, a science *a priori*, so far as it still refers to objects, and may be applied to them. For instance, it is a transcendental cognition, that Space is a perception a priori, and yet is applicable to sensible objects. The *transcendental* is opposed to the *empirical*, which latter not only relates to, but likewise arises from, experience.

TRUTH—*Wahrheit*

is the agreement or coincidence of our cognition, 1) with itself, i. e. its own characters, and with the general rules of thought: 2) with its objects; and hence material, positive, *objective*, real, synthetical truth, reality. It requires, that the object be given; the principle of contradiction is only a negative criterion of truth.

UNCONDITIONAL or UNCONDITIONATE—*Unbedingt*,

that, which is absolutely and in itself, i. e. internally possible, which is exempt from those conditions, that circumscribe a thing in Time and Space. Such is the idea of human Reason in the most extensive sense, as it is capable of continual improvement, which, although it cannot be realized in experience, is unlimited; the sphere of the objects of cognition being boundless. And this circumstance ought not to deter, but rather to encourage us in our exertions for the attainment of knowledge, which may be carried on *in indefinitum.*—Compare this Article with the term 'CONDITIONAL.'

GLOSSARY.

UNDERSTANDING—*Verstand*

1) in the most extensive sense, is the self-active faculty of cognition (spontaneity), or the faculty of producing representations, of uniting the representations given or perceived, of thinking and judging upon objects:

2) in particular; the faculty of forming conceptions and judgments of objects perceived; the faculty of acquiring experimental cognitions, i. e. of forming rules, as opposed to laws. In this sense, the Understanding is distinguished from Reason in a more limited signification.

The WILL

1) in general, is the arbitrary determination, the causality of a living being, the power of producing objects corresponding with conceptions, or at least of determining oneself as to the attainment of them; an appetitive faculty in general;

2) in particular, the causality of Reason with respect to its actions, practical Reason and Liberty; a faculty of acting conformably to principles, i. e. to the representation of laws—to produce something, that corresponds with an idea or purpose.

WISDOM—*Weisheit*

is the idea of the necessary unity of all possible purposes. It is therefore 1) *theoretically* considered, the cognition of the highest good: 2) *practically*: an attribute of that will, which realizes the highest good, or at least exerts itself for that purpose.

FINIS.